THE REAL
TREE
OF
LIFE

THE REAL TREE OF LIFE

HOW YOU CAN HAVE THE FRUIT OF LIFE...
AND PROSPER

WILLIAM R. JACKSON

THE REAL TREE OF LIFE
HOW YOU CAN HAVE THE FRUIT
OF LIFE... AND PROSPER

Scripture quotations from the Holy Bible, King James Version (Authorized Version). First published in 1611. Quoted from the KJV Classic Reference Bible.

NCV
Scripture quotations marked "NCV" are taken from the New Century Version, Copyright © 1987, 1988, 1991 by Word Publishing, a division of Thomas Nelson, Inc. Used by permission. All rights reserved.

NIV
Scripture quotations marked NIV are taken from the Holy Bible, New International Version®. NIV®. Copyright © 1973, 1978, 1984 by International Bible Society. Used by permission of Zondervan. All rights reserved. [Biblica]

iUniverse books may be ordered through booksellers or by contacting:

iUniverse
1663 Liberty Drive
Bloomington, IN 47403
www.iuniverse.com
1-800-Authors (1-800-288-4677)

Because of the dynamic nature of the Internet, any web addresses or links contained in this book may have changed since publication and may no longer be valid. The views expressed in this work are solely those of the author and do not necessarily reflect the views of the publisher, and the publisher hereby disclaims any responsibility for them.

Any people depicted in stock imagery provided by Getty Images are models, and such images are being used for illustrative purposes only. Certain stock imagery © Getty Images.

ISBN: 978-1-5320-7883-5 (sc)
ISBN: 978-1-5320-7882-8 (e)

Print information available on the last page.

iUniverse rev. date: 08/06/2019

"The Multi-colored Wisdom of God"

– Joseph Sarkesian
North Georgia

CONTENTS

ACKNOWLEDGMENTS

Much of my life I've dreamed greatly, and an even greater dream altogether to ever thought that I would write about some of the things I felt about life, and how it should be lived through my lively-hood experiences.

As I sat back and rationalized the way of life––the good and bad––the way I viewed it or in so believed it to be, these views have actually become my focus to DO better every moment in this life, and to share these discoveries with others.

Before I began this book in the year of 2008, I gave it much thought–figuring that, who wants your information that began from little hand-out of pieces of paper? Like everything else, we must try, experiment as layman scientist, and see what happens. Isn't that what lives are all about, experimentation? Another part of life!

In not forgetting that simple thing "belief" or is it that simple? But I understand that it (belief) can, and is in many of our lives a hindrance, and it is that I began every thought and action with belief as my core foundation, and the ultimate belief, believes in self!

Belief in self determines whether you achieve anything in your life in one day, one month, or years after–or nothing at all. Belief in self "I think" can be used as a measuring tool to determine your personal accomplishments i.e., the more you belief in self, the more you will accomplish. Additionally, encouragement is always helpful, but I find that no matter what, it takes belief in yourself because of course, this is your life. And, what you make of it will ultimately determine how one measured to the dash between his/her time of birth, and final time of death. And so, it bores down too, how would we like to be remembered???

The Spirit and people I would like to acknowledge here are those that have either given me Grace, inspiration—whether conscious or unconsciously of their actions:

YAHWEH, of who I've finally placed all my confidence in, and unyielding faith. The One, that gave me something to work with as simple evangelical messages before entrusting my responsibility in a thing as a book. I thank You, and I praise You for Your Grace bestowed upon me.

Irissa, my mother, who is a true believer and worshipper of our living God, exhibited her virtuousness altogether without selfishness. Always exemplified that I do not owe her, nor anyone else anything, nothing, zilch, but only God, because His Power and Words are the answer my life success. And ... my step-father Ozzie, of whom of nearly forty-years and counting are the foundation of the family, and I credit him to be my father. Good man and I thank you.

Ms. Laura Fountain, a Counselor at a State Department of Corrections, of who at the beginning of the evangelical messages, assisted me, and offered wonderful ideas.

Ms. Donna Payne, an Administrative Assistant, also with the Department of Corrections, inspired me more than ever through her leadership in Common Ground (straight talk) Mentor Class. She unknowingly, gave me motivation to continue writing the little messages every week that ignited my thinking capacity about the many issues we face in our society, which now, has developed into a book. She is a wonderful and very sincere person. The population of inmates, serving time in Georgia, of which if it were not them expecting the messages every week, then possibly this book would not BE. But our Higher Power knows the outcome. But their kind words of thanks, and positive comments meant more to me than the messages probably aided them. But for both of us, it is a product that is immeasurable. Special thanks to Richard B. Glass, of whom listened to any idea that came to my mind unwavering. Kevin Gooch, of who confronted me every week as if I owed him money, anticipated me supplying him with a weekly word of wisdom. Richard Bailey, who read, and saved every message since day one, Christopher Bass, and all these guys following were the principle anticipators of a good word: Raleigh McKenzie, Tim Lee, Charles Marshal, this guy is something else; Randy McGee, Todd Griffen, Larry Middlebrooks, Bobby Herz, John Lash, Patrick Pearson, Phillip Yarbrough, John Mallard, Ricky Thomas, Larry Schneider, Kerry Shirley, Juan Arreguin, Reginald L. Brown, Jeffery Mills, Quinton Thompson, Michael Scott, Charles Asherbranner, Eric Kelly, of whom I expect to be a very successful man; Kenyatta Cosby, Ricky Alexander, Johnny Lovain, Aaron Elders, a real character; Charles Mize, Shawn Greiner, John Bennett, Howard Williams, Roy Kilgore/Anthony Kilgore, of whom are not of any relation; Ociel Pineda, Juan Sanchez, Jorge Perez, Felimon Muñoz, and the rest of the *familia*.

And last, but not least, all other persons I may have forgotten and surely not intentionally, please forgive me, and if you know that I may have forgotten you, and you have my best interest at heart, a space below is provided for your signature. I thank you all from the depth of my heart.

PREFACE

HOW YOU CAN HAVE THE FRUIT OF LIFE... AND PROSPER

Describing the lesser-side (negative), lowest and scum-bag of society is what the finger-pointers labels just-a-bout anyone who is arrested, convicted, and sentenced of nearly any criminal act nowadays. Me, I rather not testify! And plead the Fifth. It's my past, and if anyone is to move forward, then, one needs not soak him or her self in negative historical episodes of their lives–if possible–as if it takes precedent in their lives being Newsworthy. The finger-pointers need to use something to redirect their wrong-doings in another direction. The only time that naive society becomes any thing nearest to reality, which I define as "truth", is when their actual commitment of a criminal act has hit home. Or, their closes relative are convicted (father, mother, son, or daughter) of a crime.

What I can share with my reader out-of-respect, is that once you've served so much, and too much time under a Life Sentence, it becomes wake-up call before you've reached one-quarter of the incarceration. I think the better part of the rehabilitation comes at the first part of the sentence-through-the seventh year, because one really puts forth most exertion of his/her energy towards changing for the better because of expectation of that first parole-review, and possible release. Bam! Boom! Dang! Denied...! At this point, all avenues suddenly are open to continue to DO wrong, or choose to continue to DO right. I've chosen to DO the right thing.

Don't confuse the above-aforementioned, as if these writings arise from a convict perspective, and all of sudden he is the philosopher of the World, and became Mr. Do-right. Wrong...! The majority of arrive at certain age and know what we are doing. But, yes, I was one that simply got caught in the web of the underworld and continuing to fight to get loose to regain my right place in society like every other Citizen of these United States. And so, the contents of this book is printed, hopefully, for ones every situation. And... for every Citizen whether Mr/Mrs DO-RIGHT, or... Mr/Mrs DO-WRONG.

It is to this day, I thank my Higher Power, for all my progress in life, and regress, because it was equally a valuable learning experience that for some, may have never confronted such choices to be made, that if so, may become a disaster for them because of inexperience of facing a detrimental situation. Again, these writings just may help ones that are being dealt a bad-hand right now. May God bestow His Grace upon you now.

I'm like most children reared by a good Christian family, a struggle here and there. No need for much. Always fed, and clothed. Most important, I was loved. What happens to many children that were never poor and not lacking love? This question does not discriminate. I've met and seen rich kids go crazy, nuts, and turn into drug and/or alcohol addicts. Middle-Class children down the street and make one wish he or she were part of that good-to-do family.

And then, to everyone's surprise! He or she just murdered the entire family, and only to say that the devil must have been in him, but no one can calculate a logical conclusion for such a hideous act. But then, I have never heard of a poor person committing such crime. No excuses for the underprivileged. But at least we can agree that "bad acts" are not discriminatory. And that good-to-Do is accessible to us all. And so again, these writings are here to help us all—in some way.

To my understanding, some of us have dust on our hearts giving us a greater opportunity for changing for the better. Some of us have dirt. Some of us mud. And some of us crust. Depending upon the thickness, is what determines who could be reached sooner, and enough softness to DO the right thing and exercise compassion, and respect the right's of others and their property.

My actual face-to-face, full 360° turn-a-round presented itself in the year of 2004. If you are one that does not realize what I'm actually saying here, let me spell it out to you. "I" call it Divine Revelation. A revelation that is not selfish. Not discriminatory. Not for a preferred race, creed, or color of a people. God is not picky. He's a multi-colored, multi-generational God, and... willing to bestow His Multi-Colored Wisdom upon any one that is humble enough to receive Him. His Word says; *"That ya'll may be the children of your Father which is in heaven: for he make his sun to rise on the evil and on the good, and send rain on the just and on the unjust.*

Matthew 5:45. NIV

I remain to this day, amazed of the achievements I continue to obtain after, and after another. What began this book started in the year of 2007, meditating upon my purpose in life, His Will, and trying to relate that, or my thoughts, or His Words to another? Then, around October of that same year, His Grace was bestowed upon me to DO Goodnewsmessaging (evangelical work) through little made-up paper strips that were not wider than 1 and a quarter of an inch, and no longer than 3 inches. That turned into distributing some kind of message geared to at least to help one person would be a job complete for that week. It became my duty–my job for the kingdom of God, and it remains my job today. They were made of mixed writings; simple words of knowledge that can relate to them–real life experiences; wisdom (philosophy), and scripture every-now-and-then that sequences with the subject. Today, those same little writings are the make-up for this book. – The book is designed for the "practice" of 1 out of the fifty-two chapters – each week. At the beginning of each chapter heading, it is the topic of the little messages that I was distributing to ones that would accept them. These messages are inserted for inasmuch, so that you will have the general idea as to how I got started, and also, the beginning of this book. I would like for you, with the utmost sincerity, to take that 1 chapter each week of your choosing, and think, contemplate, and meditate upon it for that week, so as to grasp the full understanding as to gather a positive result "for you", because everyone usually have their own opinion, for if it concludes a positive result, then that message has completed its task. There is also a "index" placed at the back of the book for a favorite word or thought that may come to your mind–if it's located within the index, search that word in every place that word may appear by its page number within the chapters. By doing this, I am confident that somewhere in these pages that there will be something that will relate to you, or your situation, someway, each day.

And last, you will find in some chapters, exercises to complete. Let me remind you that, it is important that you go through these simple exercises. I thank you, and may God compliment (bless) your life as He has done for me day-after-day.

THE
PRACTICE

1

WHAT IS YOUR LIFE?

Okay... my friend! When you were born into this World, the **only** things you've come to **know,** are what every person, place, or thing has taught you or... wanted you to know. On the other-hand, since you are grown-up–you're in control now huh?––Mr. Know It... But its funny how everything in and of this World existed before you–you're playing catch-up no matter what. The question is then... **What Is Your Life???**

This came to my mind after acknowledging others––I included, that, we actually think we are in control of everything––I thought! Oh, how it is now that you should see as I. Can you deal with reality? If cannot, then, I think you should really start examining yourself––inside!

EXERCISE: Step outside for at least five-minutes. Look around you and gaze in the direction that you may observe the greatest of distance. What do you see? And how far did you see?

If you have done like I asked, then, like I, there was nothing much you seen that you haven't noticed before. And of course, you probably couldn't survey any more than a half-a-mile.

I've had the opportunity to have traveled many places, and just in these United States alone will make you a dot of just one of the thousands upon thousands of species that survive in North America. And, compared to the World—you're nothing! Oops! Sorry about the touch of reality. For the person that has no idea about the size of the World, I suggest that if you own a computer, do a little research to discover the magnitude of Earth. If you do not possess a computer, then, search the encyclopedia, or maybe a dictionary. Additionally, you may discover how long Earth existed before you. I, myself, continue to be amazed of this phenomenal World we live in, and I have come to respect it. But, all of a sudden, a massive majority of people reap the opportunity to breathe the Spirit (air) of Life, and astoundingly, you, they, we, become Mr. or Mrs. Know-it-all. Not declaring that you are worthy to be of value, or valuable, there is a difference here.

The root word of valuable is *value* as a plural noun, which means:

Principles or Standards the accepted principles or standards of an individual or a group.

According to the "value" definition is *accepted principles or standards that makes one valuable,* and one valuable possession we all should have as a core value *(See also;* chapter on core value; respect, which is *the appreciation or regard for the "value" of something or someone.")*.

So is it fair for me to conclude that it's not all about you, but the appreciation or regard for something or others. This is how you have the opportunity to catch-up and join the World to become an important part of it. It can educate you on much that you need to *know.* This reminds me of something my Grandfather J. P. Davis, once told me. He said; "Once you become to *know* Nature, then you'll become to *know* life." Don't wait until you're old and gray to begin to understand the above-aforementioned as I have done at the age of forty-two, which was in the year of 2002. And so it has come to this question again, what is you're...Life?

2

LIFE OF YOUR HANDS

What if a producer were to film and tell your story based on the life of your hands? What would you see? As with us all, the film would begin with an infant's fist, then of a tiny hand wrapped around mommy's finger. Then what? Holding on to things as you learned to walk? ... Your movie is viewed by family, friends, and other, you are proud of certain moments: your hands offering gifts, placing a ring on your bride's finger, doctoring a wound, preparing a meal. ... And then there are other scenes. ... Hands taking more often than giving, demanding instead of offering.... Oh, the power of our hands. Leave them unmanaged and they become weapons: clawing for power, strangling for survival, seducing for pleasure. But manage them and our hands become instruments of grace—not just tools in the hands of God, but Gods very hands.

> *But those who do right will continue to do right, and those whose hands are not dirty with sin will grow stronger.* **JOB 17:9, NCV**

EXERCISE: I want you to try this exercise as I have done before. Stare at, and examine your hands for moment. Seriously! After have completing the examination, sequencing, meditate about your hands with them placed behind your back without them touching together with your eyes closed for at least 3-minutes. (Or for as long as you want.) Then open your eyes with your hands remaining behind your back. Read-on below:

Yes, you are conscious that you have a pair of hands, but, do you see them? You definitely should not, because they should have remained behind your back. Now, think about how a person feels absent their hands, or even maybe their entire arms excluded from their bodies, up too their shoulders? Now, think about how God has complimented (blessed) you to have arms, and able usage of them. And then, think about how we take that blessing and misuse and abuse our hands—even our entire bodies. This reminds me of the Written Words of Divine Revelations, stated as follows:

> *For you created my inmost being; you knit me together in my mother's womb. I praise you because I am fearfully and wonderfully made; your works are wonderful, I know that full well. My frame was not hidden from you when I was made in the secret place. When I was woven together in the depths of the earth, your eyes saw my unformed body. All the days ordained for me were written in your book before one of them came to be. How precious to me are your thoughts, O God! How vast is the sum of them! Were I to count them, they*

> *would outnumber the grains of sand. When I*
> *awake, I am so with you.*
> **Psalms 139:13-18, NIV**

I don't know about you, but after I attentively read that verse, and then over again, I gave my LORD a hallelujah of praise. It is a wonderful revelation to me to know how much my Father in the Heavens molded me, and with protection. If you have received any part that Multi-colored Wisdom of God, in which I am trying to convey this revelation (reveal or make known) too your life, you would have began your attempt to humble yourself today.

There is a multiple-billion of people on this Earth. (*See also;* the chapter of Claiming To Be... Alright?) And you think you are the better one out of all those billions. That's literally funny! Realities check again! And instead of you thanking and praising The Supreme Architect for bestowing His Grace upon you, for molding you wholly––tip to toe–– top to bottom, with every functioning part as what we know of to having a whole and complete body, and you probably even have the nerves to look-down on one missing a limb or two. I hope not!

Thank God, or Who ever you praise, for your hands now. And start today by managing them better to DO good works.

> *But those who do right will continue to do*
> *right, and those whose hands are not dirty*
> *with sin will grow stronger.* **JOB 17:9, NCV**

3

SPENDING YOUR TIME

Spending your time imagining what would have been if you could have changed some little thing, some little decision in your life, is counterproductive and leaves you unhappy. Think about how you can improve for the future, but don't waste the present thinking about how you could have changed the past.

I believe I have earned the right to put in the picture these next words. If you have never been incarcerated over more than 3-days before, it is really a total waste of your time––absolutely counterproductive for you to think that if you could have changed some little thing, some little decision in your life. I tell you now, you cannot change the past, but you have all the strength to improve for the future––inasmuch if you have not ciphered it away with them ridiculous thoughts.

Take a man or woman that has served twenty or more years in prison. I know, I know... you are probably saying that, "they shouldn't have done what they did to end-up there. And ... if you can do the crime, then they should do the time." You're partly right, but yep! That's the typical right-wing Citizens reply––until it hits home. Instead of you accepting it as an antidote to assist you in being even a more productive, happy and joyful person, you've already forgotten about the principle subject––Spending Your Time.

The truth is, it's amazing how one can adjust to about any situation when subjected too it. Meaning, after a person is convicted and sentenced, usually, at the average of about six-to-eight months after arrest, and then shipped-off to prison, you'll be very surprised how he/she has excepted it and apt to improve his/her future. Yes, it becomes natural from time-to-time to drift off towards what is happening in society, but the mind becomes trained to dwell in the busyness of planning, thinking, setting dreams and goals––and some end-up being unrealistic because they are not supplied with all of the technical tools needed to analyze, and collectively produce a plan(s) that will result to improvements after release. But, you'll also be surprised that the aforementioned is the norm from at least five-through-twenty or more years.

Now, let's refer to you, and it will be short. Do you waste your time thinking about some little thing of the past–– especially that has not landed you in prison for 5-to-20? If so, then you need to change your entire surroundings. Get a new husband or wife, change communities, your job, and pray because you have problems. You have opportunities prisoners are willing to kill for––just kidding there! But seriously, a majority of prisoners think, think, think all their time through, pray and wish for their next chance to liberty––which most will get, so they can do the right thing that "they feel" they did not have the opportunity to DO. It is not made newsworthy of the successful releases––only the bad ones are reported and made newsworthy because of political reasons. And for one that never been to prison and released, it is no wonder why you believe what you believe.

Spend your time productive, and enjoy it before you regret it. You only have one life!

4

BUSY IS BETTER
THAN BORED

Find something Good to DO, because feeling that we have too much to do is much more pleasing (revelrous) than feeling we have nothing to DO.

> *Let us not grow weary while Doing good, for in due season we shall reap (gather) if we do not lose heart.* **Gal. 6:9, NKJV**

How often do you hear one complaining about their hectic schedule? It's always I'm tired, give me a break, I need more hours in a day, what do they expect me to do, Jesus! Why me? So on, and so on.

Why not you? Believe me; try giving up every duty that you've taken responsibility for, and I can about guarantee that you'll feel you are going crazy by not Doing nothing. Just within me, thinking, about not Doing anything is a terrible feeling. Oh yes, I will just stop writing because it's too much. Please... give me a break! Oh, did I just say–– Give Me A Break? Don't confuse the issue here. For my direct-statement is meant as to say; "you can leave me alone, because I have work to do."

What I would like you to reflect upon is why do we have strength??? Some times we even pray for it. It is for every food we consume is purposed for a reason. I will not give every detail to these supplements are for our daily diet, but I will say that also, eating is a Doing thing, and ... quite a must. From the time we awake until rest is a step toward reaping what we sow.

Most do not understand the meaning of work, which is such a beautiful thing. Work: is the exertion of physical or mental energies.

Nature is so incredible! Don't you know our bodies (physical), and the brain (mental) are at work while we're sleeping? It is actually exerting energy a tidy-bit, but in a switching mode of gathering (reaping) energy while at rest. In the moments of awaking, energy is being exerted, and the more active we are, the more exertion of that physical or mental energies. This does not take any employment to exert your energy. It is whether playing, walking, skipping, waving, talking, thinking, visioning, and you name it. Anything the body or mind does exerts energy. Now, what it bores... down too, is how you plan to exert your energy through a day. You can choose to exert it in a negative way, and doing nothing, as you think, is actually negative. Or, you can choose to exert your energy in a positive way. The more you use your energy in a positive manner; this is Revelrous to Good, and pleasing to your soul, because you will gain all life's fulfillments.

Because you understand the difference between Doing something, and not doing, now you're able to reap a more happy and joyful life. You are pleased with your job or business that supports you or your family. You are now willing and ready to DO for your family, relatives, and friends. Now, everything and everybody around you are happy souls. Doing something is on your No. 1 list now. *(See also;* The Similarities in Life and Baseball.)

> *Let us not grow weary while Doing good, for in due season we shall reap (gather) if we do not lose heart.* **Gal. 6:9**

5

SMALL DREAMS...
MEDIUM DREAMS...
BIG DREAMS...

It doesn't matter the size of a **dream**--how short or how long it may take to manifest. There are very few individuals born with the silver spoon, but the majority accomplished **Dreams** by **Doing** what needed to be done.

> For a **dream** comes through much activity (work), And a fool's voice is known by his many words. **ECC. 5:3 KJV**

The chapter preceding this one we discussed how important it was to DO. This chapter discusses your DREAMS--matter of fact, you will find throughout these chapters mentioning the simple two-letter word; DO! I cannot emphasize enough how important the word "DO" is.

Let's discuss why I emphasize how important the word "DO" is. The "DO" affects your entire life from the very small things, too the much larger things. Not Doing from the start of the very small things through much larger things, can and will stunt any desired DREAM, you dreamed of doing. How can you reap what you sow, that if you are a person who thinks, or do not exert the energy needed to become pleased from the "work" you have done?

Take a home-garden created by you in your back yard for instance. Actually, that garden seems so simple too you, that you feel it doesn't need much work. Wrong! What you really did was create and produce a Small Dream that didn't take much work. But whatever the size of the dream, always takes planting the seed (planning), watering that seed (managing or overseeing the operations). After it has grown, then you can consume it (production). Whether small, medium, or BIG DREAMS are based by the same system, but more energy exerted (mentally and physically) by the bigger the task. If you do not have any health problems, then I offer not excuses anyone, but one, and we'll get to that in a moment. Besides that one that we will discuss below, other than that, there is not any other reason why you cannot have your DREAM come true. The information I will supply below, may, or may not apply to you.

Before I state my claim, I want to assure you that I am not any psychologist, sociologist, or stating any facts that any professional has accepted as facts. But what I am about to share with you comes from my life experiences, personal studies, progressive wisdom, and my faith in what I have received from the written words of divine revelations that has and continued to help me.

Ask yourself, from birth, and until you have become so-called independent from mom and dad, how did you acquire what you know now? Provided below are a list of things I want you to place a check (ü) by each one that relates too you.

1. As you discovered, from birth and until at least 3-years-old, you were taught everything by your mother, father, sister and brothers (if any).
2. Around 4-years-old (pre-k), you were learning from the family, a baby-sitter, or enrolled into pre-school.
3. Around 5 or 6-years-old, you were learning from the family, a baby-sitter, and/or kinder garden school.
4. At 6-years-old, until at least 12-years-old, you were learning from the family, a baby-sitter, other kids, grade school, and a number of Communication Networks.
5. From around 13-years-old, and until at least 18-years-old, you were learning from family, friends, associates, grade and High School, and a number of Communication Networks.
6. From 18-years-old, and until this day, you learn some things from family, friends, associates, perhaps College, and numerous Communication Networks.

If you missed checking any of them specified above, you failed, or simply do not want to accept these facts. But the truth is, in America, it is no way you can escape the way we're taught in this society, or get around the system of things. But these next lines will probably surprise you. And adding to that, you're apt not to believe it anyway, but it's okay, because its your life–the way in America it is also, that people raised and not believe in themselves.

From your beginning of life, you were taught by people who believed and learned the way you have. It is the same for them; they learned the same thing from others that taught them. Nothing has changed. At least eighty-five-percent of the people born and reared in America have the same belief. Nearly five-percent of the eighty-five-percent believed enough to change a thing a little-bit toward their belief. And so, there is a name-change or two. A few different words or so, but the total picture is viewed the same. You cannot tell me that you had not believed in the Tooth Fairy, Old Santa Claus, Mr. Easter Bunny, Valentines Day, and you name it? Oh yea, now you don't! But you do not realize that you remain to believe in those things unconsciously, because you still teach your children the same belief. And in addition to that, you cannot stop basking yourself in the Celebrations–– because everyone you know believes the same, and its how it's done, Right? The reason why it affects your DREAMS, is because of all the fantasizing, miraculous embedded thoughts, symbolism, and so on that has saturated your life, and not allow reality to soak in enough through your belief system for the actual manifestation of your DREAM come true. How can you have anything come "true", if all your life been taught falsehood? I will be honest with you because that's my life, now! Honesty; is the measure of how you treat TRUTH.

You may be surprised, but I still Celebrate the falsehood today as well. But the difference between me and you is that I "know" falsehood, and accept this in my life as such only to celebrate the joy of it but, I do not "believe" it. I relate these things to my children, family, friends, and any others of who might try to seduce me with falsehood. And by that, it leaves the door open to reality. I believe in self. I believe in anything you DREAM to do or have, you can DO it.

When they say; "America the Dream", there is much truth to that, because it's actually the way people in this Country are raised. Watch them at times, study them. Why can other people come to this Country and all-of-a-sudden are Doing well? It's because they're not reared upon dreams. Their reared upon reality, and if you define reality––it's defined as TRUTH. You can be who you want to BE.

> *For a dream comes through much activity (work), And a fool's voice is known by his many words.* **ECC. 5:3**

6

CHOICES...

You've come to the end of the road, which DO you turn?

RIGHT -v- **LEFT**
Love –v- hate
Joy –v- sadness
Peace –v- war
Longsuffering –v- no patients
Gentleness –v- harsh
Goodness –v- bad
Faith –v- unbelief
Meekness –v- non-compliance
Temperance –v- no control
SUCCESS –or- **FAILURE**

But if serving the LORD seems undesirable to you, then choose for yourselves this day whom you will serve. **JOS. 24:15 NIV**

It's no wonder why this Country is in so much turmoil–– there is a vast amount of disarray. The people, the citizens of this Country, I cannot totally place the blame on. The question is then, who do you blame?

Yes, in America, the Government can be partly the blame. I will not elaborate into the depth of their involvement, but I will comment on two (2) things. (1), for instance, if you have had bad and abusive parents, would you want to do as they do? I hope your answer is No! And (2) do not take everything said or done as face value. You need to question just about every official there is that represents you––including, spiritual, economic, and educational leaders. With all the propaganda and lies, you need to look seriously at the other-side of the story, and then you just might discover the truth.

So, how can you battle all the demons in America? First, you need to slow-down, step-back, and wait, (*See;* the chapter on slow-down, step-back, and wait) because you're answers come when you meditate before making a move. This is why the Written Word of Divine Revelation emphasizes longsuffering (patience).

Its time for you to BE responsible for every action *you* do. Meaning, self-govern yourselves, though you really think that you do already. Most of us cannot be governing self if that you seek government assistance in most everything you do, or need help when some disaster occurs. If we had so many *true Christians,* we would assist each other. And every time one commits a crime, of course he or she subjects themselves to the Government. Believe me, if one practice's and apply each *fruit of the spirit* (Galatians 5:22, 25), then, and not until then, that you'll be on your way to self-governing yourselves. You will BE-gin to make all the right *choices* for yourself, and family. This is the difference between *success* and *failure.* Remember, Nature has two-sides to every story. Try examining every thing you possibly can, and see if you can discover the opposite-side of it. For example, boy and girl, positive and negative, up and down, man and woman, so on. Read Ecclesiastes Chapter 3, *The Times.*

> *But if serving the LORD seems undesirable to you, then choose for yourselves this day whom you will serve.* **JOS. 24:15 NIV**

7

THEM O... TROUBLES

The fact is, bad times really are like storms. They flood in and knock you down, and it can seem like they're going to sweep away everything good in your life. But eventually the waters subside.

George Foreman
Ex-Boxer

The righteous cry out, and the LORD hears them; he delivers them from all there **troubles. Psalms. 34:17 KJV**

The words above, used within my earlier evangelism days are an excerpt from a story by the ex-boxer, George Foreman, printed by the *Guideposts* magazine, except for the verse which is from the King James Bible.

The excerpt of Mr. Foreman, had inspired me greatly, and I felt my spirit leading me to help spread the wisdom of Mr. Foreman, for the kingdom of God.

What have actually opened-up mine eyes, is how much the Written Words of Divine Revelation use much symbolism––like the *storm* that can be used as a representation of our bad times. Symbolism; which is a thing, or something said, that could mean something else. Christ, used symbolism constantly in reference to the stories (messages or sermons, evangelizing), that he was persistently tried to convey too many people as, the rich, poor, sinners, and spiritual, economic and political leaders. This symbolism is called: Parables. When one becomes able to discern the parable, story, illustration, or symbolic meaning, and compare it to his/her life, then they become much better off, and much more closer to understanding the wisdom that God wants each and every human in this World to possess.

If you can actually understand the words of George, and of Christ about the Storm, then, it will actually assist you through your bad times. When I say, *understand,* I am saying; to perceive, comprehend, to KNOW, to grasp, and feel what a storm is about. When you can perceive these things, then it will simply come to you, that; *okay, this is a category 1, 2, 3, and so on. Okay, it's a five (5), a terrible situation here. I can feel it, they can feel it,* we *can feel the turbulence of this disaster (storm), but this is how we will handle this thing or two, with prayer. This is a big test of our faith, so let's congregate, pray, support one another, because we are complimented (blessed) just simply to be living.*

Now, the storm has passed, and all has lighten-up (water subsided) and we can start rebuilding our lives. We've found new jobs, momma is recovering from the operation and doing great, we were able to afford new transportation, the church has supplied us enough food to last until things get better, the community got together to help us prepare the roof on the house, Oh God, thank You for Your Grace that has empowered the Banker to grant us the loan we needed to continue the operations of the family business, Jesus Christ, thanks for the intercession in our behalf to bring John home in one piece from the war.

Above are the many storms we face in our lives. It will never cease to be apart from our lives, for as long as the wind blows, it is eminent a storm will enter our lives. Through our faith, we must battle that storm because the good will come around next. And if you have joy when things are going great, then hold onto your joy when things get ruff, because good and bad are first cousins, one or the other will ultimately show-up at your door one way or another. Them O... Troubles are life.

> *The righteous cry out, and the LORD hears them; he delivers them from all there* ***troubles.*** **Psalms. 34:17 KJV**

8

INTELLIGENCE

According to the definition of intelligence below, are we really intellectual human-beings, or just plain *dumb animals* that are trained to act accordingly? **Intelligence: 1. a.** The capacity to acquire and apply knowledge. **b.** The faculty of thought and reason. c. Superior powers of mind.

> *Be careful what you think, because your thoughts run your life.* **Proverbs 4:23 KJV**

The Written Word of Divine Revelation in Genesis-the Beginning; "Let us make man in our image." Image: *noun.* 1. A reproduction of the form of someone or something, esp. a sculptured likeness. I don't know about you, but if you believe in the Written Word of Divine Revelation, then you ought to believe your Father in the Heavens has said. For me, I am in His image. He wants me to Be a duplicate, an example after Him. Though I am not THE GOD, but I am in His image, then what does that make me? You figure it out for me and you. When you come-up with the answer, believe me, it's a start toward big change in your life. If you choose to BE as your Father in the Heavens, then you choose to DO all the right things for yourself, your family, and others. You choose not, then, to BE a plain dumb animal, trained to act accordingly to the system of this World. Yes, you participate in the lying, cheating, and disrespect of human life. Greed is your life. No matter what, I got to get me attitude, as they say. Take another mans life without regret. A sexual predator-you name it. Even if you decide or plan to BE a slave, bondservant at one mans empire (place of employment) forever––and nothing is forever––then you do not choose to BE in the image of your Father in the Heavens, because He's given everyone the opportunity to *create,* and progress in this life and not stunt your growth in prosperity. But the ultimate gift He's provided from His image is intelligence.

Intelligence: 1. a. The capacity to acquire and apply knowledge. b. The faculty of thought and reason. c. Superior powers of mind.

Do you really acknowledge the definition of *intelligence?* Animals do not have this capacity, and do not act like we do, except for the natural animal instincts to eat only when they are hungry. Attack when they are threatened. But we tend to act worse than animals. We damn near kill anything–– including a human-being for a sport. I don't even want to elaborate any further on the stupidity of the human-being *in this chapter* because we are a very sad species. Just think we're even capable of incarcerating people for longer than normal, like caged animals for a profit, or for the purpose of acquiring, and to hold an official seat. But our end is near. And if it is to end as said, then I look forward to it, because we need to start over again. Something has gone entirely wrong!

If you only knew how wonderfully you were made, maybe, just maybe it might have you to choose for the betterment of your life, and view it different.

The depth of your make-up is too vast for to go into the information. It will lead me out-of-the-way, from this books intentions, so I request that you research and study on your own, specifically, the brain. The reason why I say the brain, because I believe the brain is the real heart of man——the controller of our body and actions. If you were to go into a coma, the brain is in a state of deep unconsciousness——not actually functioning, and therefore, the rest of your body can not react and lay dormant until you awake——if you ever awake. You may continue to breathe and have a heart beat, And therefore, in reality your *actual heart,* is actually doing what that it was designed to do——pump blood. It stops, and then you will become a dead soul. And so, I will only discuss below the most important make-up of the brain, and you can use this information for further research.

The limbic system; collectively, portions of the thalamus, hypothalamus, hippocampus formation, amygdalate, caudate nucleus, septum, and mesencephalon make up a functional unit of the brain called the limbic system. These structures are linked together in a unique way by fiber pathways (could this be where the idea of fiber-optic-cable come from?) and, as a result, control multifaceted behavior, including emotional expression, seizure activity, and memory storage and recall. There is so much more to discover about you brain, and I advise you too, then also it may add to how you may start choosing your next actions in your life.

> *Be careful what you think, because your thoughts run your life.* **Proverbs 4:23 KJV**

9

PHILOSOPHY

The ancient Greek philosopher Heraclitus wrote the following lines.

A VOICE FROM ANCIENT GREECE

One cannot step twice into the same river,
for the water into which you first stepped has
flowed on.

Heraclitus

Let's begin by discovering what the word *philosophy* means. Phi-los-o-phy: *noun.* Derives from the Greek word; philo–– Having a strong affinity or preference for; loving: which means love. Sophic, which means wisdom. So, you can say that *philosophy* means, The Love of Wisdom. Or, as *The Second College Edition, the American Heritage Dictionary* describes it; 1. a. love and pursuit of wisdom...

This, you may say, the words used earlier in this text; The Multi-Colored *Wisdom* of God, are the *love of wisdom* that God wants to share amongst all races, gender, and cultures. If you are in pursuit of a happy and joyful, moral life for you and your family, this is why the Written Words of Divine Revelation was written and handed-down amongst us for generations, and generations to come. It is also why it is written, that "Wisdom is the *principle* thing; therefore get wisdom. And in all your getting, get *understanding*." Proverbs 4:7

Throughout the Written Words of Divine Revelation, is the Multi-Colored Wisdom of God. We can conclude that wisdom is none other than philosophy. That philosophy is none other than the *love of wisdom*––the wisdom, that Yahweh loves for us to pursue and obtain it through understanding. There are actually many millions of people of who not have any understanding of The Script. But right there is their lack of wisdom. They think studying themselves to be approved only extends to Bible studies and no where else of study. Again, lack of wisdom! To pursue wisdom, is like a walk through the jungle, there is not trees alone in your path, there are bugs and many other species big and small, visible and unseen. Let's not forget light and darkness. The jungle of life is a learning process, *(See;* the chapter Where does Your Journey Leads You?) and one cannot discover the actions of sinner (s) if he/she is just sitting and studying only so Bible, and only amongst the congregation. Here, I find that in this way only, your discovery of a sinner (s) can only be found amongst the Congregation, and that's just like a disease waiting to spread. The next thing the whole (holiness) church is affected with sin.

Real studies, to obtain wisdom, and the infinity of understanding, means discovering the jungle of life (the world).

> *Hear, my son, and receive my sayings, And years of your life will be many. I have "taught" you in the way of wisdom; I have "led" you in the right "paths." (paths, not just one path or road) When you "walk", your steps will not be hindered, And when you "run", you will not stumble. Take firm hold of "instruction" (the lessons or directions), do not let go; keep her, for she is your life.* Proverbs 4:10-13 NIV

Believe me, wisdom does not come through the saying; "Oh, I read my Bible every morning", but you don't research any word, time or place of history, where the word derived from––because *you should know* that the Bible did begin in the English languish, but, in what languish? You find the answer!

And so, what does the philosophical words of *Heraclitus* means too you? "One cannot step twice into the same river, for the water into which you first stepped has flowed on."

First, if we made use of the wisdom, and understood it, it would direct us down the right path. This way, once we've stepped into the river of water, and it has flowed on, then we would not have to worry about the past, or try to step into the water twice. The past has passed.

10

THANKSGIVING

Many moons ago it was celebrated as a harvest festival. Pilgrims and Native Americans first celebrated it in the early 17th century. Let's **Celebrate Thanksgiving 365 days a year.**

... Give thanks in all circumstances. **1 Th. 5:18 NIV**

Don's get me wrong, I love America. I was born and raised on this land. But what don't like, is to be fooled. I feel I have been deceived most of my life, cheated and the like, after I started researching the history of America, and just about everything else that goes along and with it, including it's Celebration of Holidays. Since, we're discussing "Thanksgiving", and then this will remain our topic.

ORIGINS:

Long before Europeans settled in North America, western Europeans observed Harvest Home festivals to celebrate the successful completion of gathering-in the season's crops. In the British Isles, Lammas Day (Loaf Mass Day), observed on August 1, was often held to celebrate a good wheat harvest. If the wheat crop was disappointing, the holiday was usually canceled.

Another important precursor to the modern Thanksgiving holiday was the custom among English Puritans (see Puritanism) of designating special days of thanksgiving to express gratitude for God's blessings. These observances were not held regularly; they usually took place only in times of crisis or immediately after a period of misfortune had passed. Puritan thanksgiving ceremonies were serious religious occasions and bore only a passing resemblance to modern Thanksgiving celebrations.

According to tradition, the first American Thanksgiving was celebrated in 1621 by the English Pilgrims who had founded the Plymouth Colony, now in the state of Massachusetts. The Pilgrims marked the occasion by feasting with their Native American guests—members of the Wampanoag tribe—who brought gifts of food as a gesture of goodwill. Although this event was an important part of American colonial history, there is no evidence that any of the participants thought of the feast as a thanksgiving celebration. Two years later, during a period of drought, a day of fasting and prayer was changed to one of thanksgiving because rains came during the prayers. Gradually the custom prevailed among New Englanders to annually celebrate Thanksgiving after the harvest.

Colonial governments and, later, state governments took up the Puritan custom of designating thanksgiving days to commemorate various public events. Gradually the tradition of holding annual thanksgiving holidays spread throughout New England and into other states. During the American Revolution (1775-1783) the Continental Congress proclaimed a national day of thanksgiving following the American victory at the Battle of Saratoga in 1777. U.S. President George Washington proclaimed another day of thanksgiving in 1789 in honor of the ratification of the Constitution of the United States. In 1817 New York State adopted Thanksgiving Day as an annual custom, and many other states soon did the same. Most of the state celebrations were held in November, but not always on the same day.

In the mid-19th century Sarah Josepha Hale, editor of Godey's Ladies Book, led a movement to establish Thanksgiving as a national holiday. In 1863, during the American Civil War (1861-1865), President Abraham Lincoln proclaimed the last Thursday in November Thanksgiving Day in order to bolster the Union's morale. After the war, Congress established Thanksgiving as a national holiday, but widespread national observance caught on only gradually. Many Southerners saw the new holiday as an attempt to impose Northern customs on them. However, in the late 19th century Thanksgiving's emphasis on home and family appealed to many people throughout the United States. As a distinctly American holiday, Thanksgiving was also considered an introduction to American values for the millions of immigrants then entering the country.

During the 20th century, as the population of the United States became increasingly urban, new Thanksgiving traditions emerged that catered to city dwellers. The day after Thanksgiving gradually became known as the first day of the Christmas shopping season. To attract customers, large retailers such as Macy's in New York City and Gimbel's in Philadelphia, Pennsylvania, began to sponsor lavish parades. By 1934 the Macy's parade, featuring richly decorated floats and gigantic balloons, attracted more than one million spectators annually.

The custom of watching football games on Thanksgiving Day also evolved during the early decades of the 20th century. As football became increasingly popular in the 1920s and 1930s, many people began to enjoy the holiday at a football stadium. Teams in the National Football League eventually established traditions of playing nationally televised games on Thanksgiving afternoon.

In 1939 U.S. President Franklin Roosevelt shifted the day of Thanksgiving from the last Thursday in November to one week earlier. Retail merchants had petitioned the president to make the change to allow for an extra week of shopping between Thanksgiving and Christmas. Many Americans objected to the change in their holiday customs and continued to celebrate Thanksgiving on the last Thursday of the month. Roosevelt's political opponents in Congress also opposed the break with tradition and dubbed the early holiday "Franksgiving." In May 1941 Roosevelt admitted that he had made a mistake and signed a bill that established the fourth Thursday of November as the national Thanksgiving holiday, which it has been ever since.

Thanksgiving is also a legal holiday in Canada. Because Canada is north of the United States, its harvest comes earlier in the year. Accordingly, the Thanksgiving holiday falls earlier in Canada than in the United States. The Canadian Parliament set aside November 6 for annual Thanksgiving observances in 1879. In 1957 the date was shifted to an even earlier day, to the second Monday in October.

Encarta Encyclopedia 99

For whatever the cause of the Celebration, always remember:
... *Give thanks in all circumstances.* **1 Th. 5:18 NIV**

11

THINK ABOUT

"The purpose of prayer is not to influence God to grant you special favors, but rather to remind yourself that you are always connected to God."

– DR. WAYNE W. DYER,
author of numerous self-help books
including
The Power of Intention

When I *think about* the above-statement by Dr. Dyer, it brings to my mind the numerous occasions that God was showing the Israelites how He was their God; how He was with them; how He was the One who would protect them. Of course, the Israelites always fell-away from Him, like rain from the skies. But most of their prayers always came in their time of trouble––if like begging for that special favor. Prayer-after-prayer when they needed Him to DO something in their time of trouble. And again, they would *disconnect* themselves from Him, until God got fed-up and said, paraphrasing; "Hey, you guy's, I've toted you along for hundreds of years, protected you, and always had compassion when you called upon my Name, but you people, I have warned you, and so I am the God of all people."

> *Come unto me, all ya'll that labour and are heavy laden, and I will give you rest.*"
> **Matthew 11:28. KJV**

God is a Multi-colored, Multi-generational God that favors all. He is our Father. No different than our earthly, biological father that raised us. Just because we became independent of mom and dad, and acquired our own home and family, that separation to next door, across the street, or them few miles we've too, did not disconnect us from our parents, but we remained *connected* to them. The same way with our Father in Heaven, we are always connected to Him. And, we should not have to be reminded of that. Your prayers is not to influence God to grant you special favors, but remind yourself that prayer is no different than calling upon, or just simply communicating with mom or dad. Try holding a conversation with your God—even if it's just to greet Him in the morning, or say goodnight, then, you'll find yourself not calling upon Him just for favors.

12

WHERE DOES YOUR
JOURNEY LEADS YOU?

"Expose yourself to as much as possible. Attend conferences no one else is attending. Read books no one else is reading. Talk to people no one else is talking to." – 19-year-old **BEN CASNOCHA,** founder of a million-dollar software company and author of *My start-Up-Life: What a (Very) Young CEO Learned on His **Journey** Through Silicon Valley.*

For the vision is yet for an appointed time. Read: HABAKKUK 2:1-3 NIV

The most educational experience I've ever had, began, and still remains to have, has derived from my travels. If you have not been taught to discover by venturing further-and-further from the cradle (home), then you are missing a glorious part of your life. How you associate, connect with the World will ultimately decide your fate, and faith in God.

One thing I can give credit too in the American Education System, is how you actually have the opportunity, after the barrier was broken, to deal and associate with the different races and cultures of people from your first start of school, until the end. If you were reluctant to start and finish school through all grades, including College, then you should not have any social problems––specifically.

Beginning now, at pre-k, and then kinder garden or first-grade was your inauguration into joining the entire weirdo's. Every little munchkin was weird, intimidating, and scary. That first day mom was about to leave you there all alone–– as you felt, because you were not one of them munchkin's from out-of-space, yet! And so, if you remembered, you were probably afraid crying and carrying-on as if you were having a heart-attack. To be honest, I did. I think my mom had to take me home with her, and gradually introduce me––while she stayed awhile, and then leave, sneakingly. Afterwards, I became the main munchkin, if not number one.

IMPORTANT MESSAGE: Remember this; I've learned that, no matter what you dislike, any time you have associated, or spent time around a thing, place, or someone for a certain amount of time, there is no doubt in my mind that you will get use to it, or them. If it's anything that is not wrong, or does not harm you, then, what the heck, check it out and learn from it. Roger!

Then, your grade-school years are always surprising when it came to starting another grade, until you gotten use to it, it's like hey, this is cool. You become entertained by all the different characters, relating does not become so hard now. You even try to become student of the year––leader in something. Now that it has become nothing to you, here is about the time you feel that you are in control and either continue your education and move onto College, or drop-out. But let's say that plan, or moved onto College.

Them, College days, that if you missed, you've missed the best part of your youthful experiences. I advise strongly, that, you enroll into College, and if you are not sure of what curriculum of study you would like, find out later after you have enrolled into something. But, hopefully after a discussion with an in-house Counselor, that you would have made a decision then. But, if not, like I said, you will eventually get use to it, discover what you really would like to study. You will come into your special group of people, that if they are serious about their education, and so, association brings on simulation. Without you're ever recognizing, you have that likeable character, able to deal with just about anyone. You're capable of delivering speeches. But I say that you are now a person that should not have a problem in progressing in life––in your finances, family, and so on. You have created for yourself the American way. Congratulations!

Now, for you that had not had the reluctance to finish grade-school, graduate from High School, then this is were you lack discipline, association, and not really knowing how to relate to others on a proper communicational basis. You most fear anyone of who went and finished school, and we won't mention College. Oh, did I mention College? Sorry! And so, you feel intimidated. This usually allows you only the low-paying job opportunities because you lack a High School Diploma, or General Education Diploma (GED). You are one, unless you are lucky, will revert toward criminal activities, and continue to play (playa)! Nothing becomes serious in your life until some thing detrimental find its way into your life, like arrest, or even prison, because you do not know how to listen to anybody. But, hopefully, if you discover perhaps, that you need to start listening and learning, maybe your life will change for the better. And most important before that, I hope you are not blaming anyone for mishaps, because if you are, you better stop-it right now and take responsibility for your own mishaps. Because I'm pretty sure you had everybody besides mom who told over-and-over to go to school.

Now, besides the above-stated and you are ready to start over, here is an antidote; if you are bounded by negative-influences, even mom or dad; the community is your down-fall, anything you feel is holding back, plan now to relocate, but most important, start a relationship with your Father in Heaven because this is where your faith is needed to face some fears you may have. Even if you fear praying because of your negative surrounding for you to do so, go pray in private where no one is around––but pray, pray, and pray. Start meditating by yourself because this is where you will receive your answers. You may say you don't have fears. Okay, if you don't, pack-up and leave mom and dad, your neighborhood, any negative surrounding right now, this minute.

FACE YOUR FEARS... because the devil will try to tell you, that you are not good enough to do better. Face your fears... because you are just as much loved by God, and many others–they just don't know how to tell you, but you are just as good as anyone else. Face your fears... because you can relate to anyone as well, just because you have not finished school, does not mean people don't like you, or even like to relate to you. Sometimes you don't hold conversations with people because you choose not too. Face your fears... just because you did not finish school, does not mean you are not capable of communicating with so-called educated people, the difference between you and them, is the use of words. What you can began to do, is start reading to enhance your vocabulary––read, read, and read. Face your fears... by exposing yourself to as much as possible. Face your fears... by traveling by yourself, increasing the distances more and more until you are not afraid to go anywhere by yourself. And last, face your fears... by praying to your God no matter who sees you, because now, it should not matter, you are a man! Or... you are a woman! Because men or women do what is responsible and good of them. Do not miss in life for what God has provided for all of us––yes, even you. Don't wait any longer because you only have one life, just like the ones you feared, so try, and try your DREAM just like everyone else until you achieve it.

See where your journey leads you!
For the vision is yet for an appointed time.
Read: HABAKKUK 2:1-3 NIV

13

CLAIMING TO BE...
ALRIGHT?

Well... it's easy for us to think that we're
the most important species on earth––like
we know it all just because we were given
dominion and the capacity to think. But,
According as his divine power have given to us
all things that pertain unto life and godliness,
through the knowledge of him that has called
us to glory and virtue: are we living? **Read**
II Peter 1:3 American KJV

We've had a discussion previously in another chapter *(See;*
What Is Your Life?) that is similar to the topic in this chapter,
but this chapter will most likely be direct, and in more depth
into and about your life.

When God gave me the revelation about the topic
Claiming To BE... Alright" for evangelizing, as a question,
it was meant to ignite the minds of the readers to actually
pose a question to himself; "is he really alright?" Whenever
I met or confronted a guy and ask him how he was doing

today, it was either one of two of the proceeding answers. One (1), most would say *alright,* or, *I'm alright;* and two (2), some acted like they were too good to be asked the question of how they were doing. But, to both, are actually bleak to real life, and who is most responsible from his birth and until his death.

I have finally confirmed within myself, that there are so many people do not realize how disconnected they are from God, or... at times for the purpose of this chapter, Nature. Remember, in the preceding chapter of *What Is Your Life,* that we discussed about how long Earth has existed, but a discussion that you were to research and come up with the answer. What was your answer for that topic? Well, if you had not done your homework, I am disappointed in you because as I continue to batter you with, it is very important to DO. You need to DO if you are going to progress in life. God does not prosper lazy people. But, the Scientist and their calculated theories have theorized that Earth has existed for nearly 4:5 billion years. Those numbers are quite hard for me to swallow, even if we accepted 1-million years. Jesus! That is still to mammoth of a number. Okay, how about breaking it down to around, let's see, to about 5,000 years, in which that still amazes me, but it at least correlates with my reality system. But, the objective of this showing of Earth existence, is to get you to see that you're not that important than ant that was created, maybe before you, simultaneously, or just after you. But, whatever, He created you not to have dominion over me, or another man, or well-defined that you, out of all His wonderful creations, that you were better than all; well I'll be damned! Wake-up!!! Any man or women, that is, or is reading this chapter, at this point. Ding-dong, ding-dong, answers the door, open it, and look yonder. What do you see? I can bet that you see trees you did not make. The flowers you have not made. What about cars? Ninety-nine-point-nine percent you didn't make it or them either. What about them streets or sidewalks? You didn't make or build them either huh. Hell, there is a great percentage that you didn't even build your own home, made the clothes you're wearing, or produced the food you and your family eats'.

What we have to open our clogged brains too, is that when and however we were made, or thrown-down or up here to Earth, that if you have done your studies of the nutrients needed, or minerals in your body, and the minerals on Earth are the same. What..., yes, I, you, Aunt Mary, Uncle Pete, grandma Sue, and all the rest of the clan is part of this Earth. It is said, that dirt we came from, dirt we will return. Below are some words that you should admire:

> *Does not wisdom call out? Does not understanding raise her voice? On the heights along the way, where the paths meet, she takes her stand; beside the gates leading into the city, at the entrances, she cries aloud: To you, O men, I call out; I raise my voice to all mankind. You who are simple, gain prudence; you who are foolish, gain understanding. Listen, for I have worthy things to say; I open my lips to speak what is right. My mouth speaks what is true, for my lips detest wickedness. All the words of my mouth are just; none of them is crooked or perverse. To the discerning all*

of them are right; they are faultless to those who have knowledge. Choose my instruction instead of silver, knowledge rather than choice gold, for wisdom is more precious than rubies, people nothing you desire can compare with her. I, wisdom, dwell together with prudence; I possess knowledge and discretion. To fear (the LORD) YAHWEH is to hate evil; I hate pride and arrogance, evil behavior and perverse speech. Counsel and sound judgment are mine; I have understanding and power. By me kings reign and rulers make laws that are just; by me princes govern, and all nobles who rule on earth. I love those who love me, and those who seek me find me. With me are riches and honor, enduring wealth and prosperity. My fruit is better than fine gold; what I yield surpasses choice silver. I walk in the way of righteousness, along the paths of justice, bestowing wealth on those who love me and making their treasuries full. YAHWEH (The LORD) brought me forth as the first of his works, before his deeds of old; I was appointed from eternity, from the beginning, before the world began. When there were no oceans, I was given birth, when there were no springs abounding with water; before the mountains were settled in place, before the hills, I was given birth, before he made the earth or its fields or any of the dust of the world. I was there when he set the heavens in

> *place, when he marked out the horizon on the*
> *face of the deep, when he established the clouds*
> *above and fixed securely the fountains of the*
> *deep, when he gave the sea its boundary so the*
> *waters would not overstep his command, and*
> *when he marked out the foundations of the*
> *earth. Then I was the craftsman at his side. I*
> *was filled with delight day after day, rejoicing*
> *always in his presence, rejoicing in his whole*
> *world and delighting in mankind. Now then,*
> *my sons, listen to me; blessed are those who*
> *keep my ways. Listen to my instruction and*
> *be wise; do not ignore it. Blessed is the man*
> *who listens to me, watching daily at my doors,*
> *waiting at my doorway. For whoever finds me*
> *finds life and receives favor from (the LORD)*
> *YAHWEH. But whoever fails to find me*
> *harms himself; all who hate me love death.*
> **Proverbs 8:1-36 NIV**

For the ones who *claim to BE... alright,* think again. Listen to this! If you continue to claim to be *alright,* keep going *al... right,* then, you'll continue to go around in circles. Do you get it? Here's a simple example: when you're driving a car, and make a right-turn, if you not attempt to sway the steering-wheel back towards the left, then, you will continue to go round-and-round, or ultimately crash into something. Got that!

> *Let your eyes look straight ahead, fix your gaze*
> *directly before you. Make level paths for your*
> *feet and take only ways that are firm. Do not*

swerve to the right or the left; keep you foot from evil. **Proverbs 4:25-27 NIV**

Claiming to BE alright when you're not, can become addictive, which is where the devil would like to be and lie. He, that Ol... devil, will stunt your growth and to have you actually thinking you are alright (fine, doing-well). Remember, he comes to steal and destroy your life. You, United States Citizen of North America, have let guards down and have been deceived.

By now, you should have humbled yourself, because this is what God wants from every person on this Earth. Even the officials are to be meek, and humble themselves. There is a deferent's between meek and humble, but most so-called Christians believe that humble yourself to authority. Yes, you do humble yourselves to *righteous* authority, but not to unrighteous and wicked authority. For it is that every man—–even authority, are to exercise meekness. When you find that authorities person is not meek (submissive, mild, gentle, compliant) in his or her ways, then you just don't humble yourself a dirty scrounge, no good, stealing-cheating, and deceiving liar, that has supposedly been placed in that position by God to serve you—–or was he placed in that position by the devil? If you have become a meek person through your reading of this chapter, and have humbled yourself towards mankind, then, you just may be on your way towards prosperity in every way bestowed upon you from God. And when this becomes you daily compassion for your brothers and sisters alike, and want for the World, then, you may have my vote. But, until you reach that height in your mind to serve your fellow man, as a Godly man, until then, we need to look, search, for these kinds of men to lead our Country. Start investigating the records of these officials before casting your vote. The men or women leading this country are only the by-product of its citizens, and visa-versa. You as crooked citizen, will vote for a crooked leader, because he's just as cunning as you, so cannot discover his or her intentions. Let me say this; this country statistically, has about eighty-two-percent of the population that confesses to believe in Christ, but about twelve-percent out-of-the nearly eighteen-percent left over are the ones running the country––the unbelievers. Now, that either tells me, that the claiming Christians in this country are not true Christians with all this destruction going on. And if they were true, then, shouldn't True Christians be running this country, if eighty-two-percent believe in Christ?

In closing this chapter, if you are *claiming to BE... alright,* then as God gave you dominion over everything except men, then rule righteously. If He appoints you a position in Government, do not abuse your position, or deceive the citizens. You are not no more important than the people you serve. I would give my life just see Jesus holding a Senate seat, or elected to the Oval Office as President of the United States, serve his functions, compared to the Bush Administration and past Presidential, Congressional, or Senatorial positions?

> *According as his divine power have given to us all things that pertain unto life and godliness, through the knowledge of him that has called us to glory and virtue:* are we living? Read
> **II Peter 1:3 NIV**

14

GOODNEWSMESSAGING

It's that time of the year where most of us incur a break in our lives, for some, it may be the end. But, for those who are living, thank God that there is a new beginning––a future, and therefore, choices we can leave behind; whether lies or truth, whether love or hate, whether same old habits or new dreams, whether irresponsibility or ability to respond appropriately to others––especially to our families, however, it is our choice, and this coming new year, let's practice making better choices. For me, I'm not perfect, but what I've learned is, if you have **good** dreams, then **DO** something to make it happen, and if its something that you like, and its **good,** then **DO** it! As for the **Goodnewsmessaging,** I love it, and I love you––for what other reason would I share a message? Remember the very first note that ended with **WHAT IS YOUR LIFE???**

How many chances do you want??? Until next year **MERRY CHRISTMAS & HAPPY NEW YEAR!!!**

When actually reviewing my evangelical hand-outs, as the one above for this book, I am like, "where did this stuff come from? I mean, I know where it comes from––thank

God, but is He actually intrusting in me to DO his work for the kingdom. Well... I see now, you bet your darn dollar He is! The reason is, as I stated before, a part of the message extracted from the above-message:

> "... As for the **Goodnewsmessaging,** I love it, and I love you—–for what other reason would I share a message?"

As you may have discovered, that that particular message was labeled *GOODNEWSMESSAGING.* It was about my break, or rest time from producing the messages because of the Christmas and New Year Holidays. Not that I was tired, or felt I needed a break, but it was not under more control to continue, and have all the available tools to continue to produce the messages. I wanted to make that clear, because I am always ready and prepared to work for God, that if it's in my power to do so.

What struck home with me the most, was, revisiting the text within that "Goodnewsmessaging" creation. I had very much felt, that as most of us at such a celebrating time of the year, many of incur a break, a vacation, or simply a time of rest. But, I felt that consuming a great deal of compassion for the ones that were not available, or ones nearing their end to celebrate with us that *I think,* the ones that had the opportunity to read that hand-out, did not notice. Though God says;

> *I am the God of Abraham, and the God of Isaac, and the God of Jacob? God is not the God of the dead, but of the living. Matthew 22:31 King James Bible*

Did you get that? I hope so, because I have. It should help us to move on, but it does not mean that we become forgetful of our love ones. It just means that, we don't have to be so caught-up in morning, sorry, and in deep thought for the ones that has left us. God is there for us who are still living. This, we should be Praising and Thanking Him. He, everyday we awake to breathe the air, we remain to be living souls and one He deserves praise. Amen!

But as God has given you another day, and another day, do you ever feel alive? Do you feel anew? Jesus! I feel everyday when I awake, and I tell you as I write this book, I feel it, and Hallelujah, hallelujah, hallelujah!

If you only knew how new your beginning is? I will not explain in depth of new you become at short intervals each year, but you'll be very surprised of how your regenerates, becoming of new to assist your health, your life, but, do you care? What a wonderful God we have. For ones that do not care, just keep living your new days, your new things, or however you think is so new. But everyone has a new opportunity—–not just when its time for a new year, but a new opportunity EVERYDAY! You choose, because that what God given you, but remember, them choices may mean life or death for every choice you make.

15

A NEW YEAR!

We focus on the **New Year;** even **celebrate** it without absolute thought of its symbolic purpose in our lives. Symbolism can be **good** if applied logically/rationally. Time, as we know it, is but a blink of an eye in the grand scheme of things. Imagine! The Earth has been here——In theory—— billions of years. Oh hell, I can't imagine that! But, lets give it 1-million; and you think your 1 to roughly 75-years, if you live that long, is so important. Who will remember you five-hundred, or twenty-thousand years from now? Find your **Good-Purpose** in life on Earth, while you have a *Gift* of a new day in the New Year, another chance for a **NEW-U.**

> **Romans 8:28 NIV ...** *God works for the good of those who love him ...* **according to his purpose.**

New Year's Day, first day of the year, January 1 in the Gregorian calendar. In the Middle Ages most European countries used the Julian calendar and observed New Year's Day on March 25, called Annunciation Day and celebrated as the occasion on which it was revealed to Mary that she would give birth to the Son of God. With the introduction of the Gregorian calendar in 1582, Roman Catholic countries began to celebrate New Year's Day on January 1. Scotland accepted the Gregorian calendar in 1600; Germany, Denmark, and Sweden about 1700; and England in 1752. Traditionally the day has been observed as a religious feast, but in modern times the arrival of the New Year has also become an occasion for spirited celebration and the making of personal resolutions. The Jewish New Year is called Rosh Hashanah, or the Feast of Trumpets, and is prescribed by the Old Testament as a holy Sabbath. It is celebrated (generally in September) on the first and second days of Tishri. The Chinese celebrate New Year's Day sometime between January 10 and February 19 of the Gregorian calendar. It is their most important holiday.

No wonder we have not, or cannot get it right. From the above information, seems every culture celebrates the New Year at different times––matter of fact, they do. And so, I see now why its so much sinful acts committed on that day. A day, that is most strictly celebrated for every thing else, that, instead of what it was really meant to be for. Then, come the day after, or come daybreak on the 1st of January, it's just a day nearly everyone is getting over headaches, and then back to the old games. Nothing new! You can see that a New Year Celebration is only symbolism. But, as mentioned in the above-evangelizing-message, that, *symbolism can be good if applied logically and rationally.*

We always need to remember that there is *nothing new* under the sun. If you actually take a serious look into reality of that so-called New Year, new day, that everybody seems to make plans for to do something new, that the majority cannot seem to accomplish, we will find that it's only a revolutionariness turn of our time. Men and women were here before us. That means, life and death, is that new? There was, and still is, night and day, is that new? No, we place a time on, and/or upon us that control our lives, that's all. Sorry, I hated to bust your bubble, but time is time just revolving in a circle. You grow older, and time suddenly changes, and that it becomes *new* to you. Haven't you ever heard of; "just live one day at a time?" Well, there is some vitality to that. *Vitality:* 1. a: the peculiarity distinguishing the living from the nonliving b: capacity to live and develop. Think about that! In extracting from the definition, it is distinguishing the living from the dead, and that living has capacity to develop. Simply live your life one day at a time, and develop as you go––develop––not underdevelopment, to do so will only enhance your capacity to join the nonliving. Other than that, there is nothing really *new* in a day, a month, or you're *New Year*.

Meanwhile, God formed us to BE creative, develop your **Good-Purpose** in life on Earth while you have a **Gift** of another day in another year to BE a **NEW-U.**

> **Romans 8:28 NIV ...** *God works for the* **good** *of those who love him ...* **according to his purpose.**

16

JOURNEY INTO DIVINE NATURE

Every person and situation in our lives is merely an "inward bound" ropes course or boulder or cliff, designed precisely to bring out the best in us–so stop complaining! Years from now, we may hardly remember the challenges or the objects of desire, fear, or anger that once seemed important enough to lie, cheat, steal or, even kill over. All we will have at the end of our lives will be the inner qualities, bad or good, which those situations gave us an opportunity to develop.

In the chapter before this one, we ended with a note about the opportunity for development, and here, in this chapter *Journey Into Divine Nature* will focus literally creating suggestions of changes and challenges, that we together hope to assist you in your developmental process.

Do you KNOW when and where your developmental process began-any idea at all? I've always been the kind of person that gives credit to when and where it was due. And so, I will admit that you've probably came very close with your answer to the above question. If your answer was, that the developmental process started through the gestation period of your mother, you were very close.

Your developmental process began when you, out of nearly five-million other sperms were in the race for life. The finish-line was the one that crossed the threshold of the protective wall of the egg that were to be fertilized. If there were two (2) or more of them squirmy little things that one cannot see with the necked eye, this is where mom became pregnant with twins, triplets, or quadruplets. The odds are very low that the aforementioned will happen, but it does every-now-and-then. Since you did not exit the womb (the day of your birth) with any other new-born, then you and I can say that, you are the winner of that race. You deserve the Gold Medal, and that alone makes you special, and do not let anyone tell you different. It was, and still is your "inward bound" ropes course. The challenges you faced began from the seconds your mother's mate (father) had had sexual relation and released his sperm for one you to fertilize the egg. Fertilization is a precise period in the reproductive process. It begins when the sperm contacts the outer surface of the egg and it ends when the sperm's nucleus fuses with the egg's nucleus. Fertilization is not instantaneous—it may take 30 minutes in sea urchins and up to several hours in mammals. After nuclear fusion, the fertilized egg is called a zygote. When the zygote divides to a two-cell stage, it is called an embryo.

Fertilization is necessary to produce a single cell that contains a full complement of genes. When a cell undergoes meiosis, gametes are formed-a sperm cell or an egg cell. Each gamete contains only half the genetic material of the original cell. During sperm and egg fusion in fertilization, the full amount of genetic material is restored: half contributed by the male parent and half contributed by the female. In humans, for example, there are 46 chromosomes (carriers of genetic material) in each human body cell–except in the sperm and egg, which each have 23 chromosomes. As soon as fertilization is complete, the zygote that is formed has a complete set of 46 chromosomes containing genetic information from both parents. And like magic, here you are–except that, it was not literally magic but, your Journey Into Divine Nature.

> *Therefore, since we are surrounded by such a great cloud of witnesses, let us throw off everything that hinders and the sin that so easily entangles, and let us run with perseverance the race marked out for us.*
> **Hebrews 12:1. NIV**

Think about it! By Nature, it was already programmed within the DNA coding a "race marked out for us" when the sperm was released. Naturally, without eyes, you ran the Marathon with over four-million others, and you are the only one finished the race. But as we've discovered, the race is not over. Many times that boulders and cliffs, we will climb, jump, hop, and skip-over. We will either let these things stop us, stunt us, slow us down, or, will we try to figure it out so that we can continue the race today–but a clean one.

> *... The race is not to the swift or the battle to the strong, nor does food come to the wise or wealth to the brilliant or favor to the learned;*

> *but time and chance happen to them all.*
> **Ecclesiastes 9:11. NIV**

Consume, with understanding, the above-written word of Divine Revelation. Life is not about how fast things are done, but the devil will trick you, as today, if like you need to be first in everything—rush, rush, rush. Or, as the young men today with their hot heads, thinks he has to show his strength through battles, whether a fist-fight or a gun. The system today has everyone believing that it takes much education to eat fine foods, to accumulate great wealth, but I tell you this, continue to run a clean race at your pace. Keep your eyes toward the prize (Jesus), and that time will happen. For life is as simple as it states below in the Written Word of Divine Revelation.

> *Go, eat your food with gladness, and drink your wine with a joyful heart, for it is now that God **favors what you DO.** Always be clothed in white (pure in mind and body), and always anoint your head with oil, enjoy life with your wife, whom you love, all the days of this meaningless life that God has given you under the sun—all your meaningless days. For this is your lot in life and in your toilsome labor under the sun. Whatever your hand finds to Do, DO it with all your might, for in the grave, where you are going, there is neither working nor planning nor knowledge nor wisdom.* **Ecclesiastes 9:7-10. NIV**

As you reap from the words of Divine Revelation through life, the many challenges, or the objects of desire, fear, or anger that many people feel to seem that it's important enough to lie, cheat, steal or, even kill over, you after many years from now, will hardly remember because you kept your eyes on the prize. You ran the race with integrity, and kept it clean. This has given you the advantage over many of them that invest in swiftness, strength, and the need of brilliancy to develop the necessities in life.

After all, when the time comes, and you have put in all your labor; Raised your children up with righteousness and respect, then, you can say; "I have fought the good fight, I have finished the race, I have kept the faith. Now there is in store for me the crown of righteousness, which the Lord, the righteous Judge, will award to me on that day–and not only to me, but also to all who have longed for his appearing." **2 Timothy 4:7,8. KJV**

17

LEADERSHIP
(THE INTRODUCTION)

When the subject of leadership entered into my spirit, and to spread as a message through evangelism, it was split into three (3) parts, which were a message of discussion to be evangelized for up to three-weeks because of the limited space I had to allow the opportunity for a greater percentage of men to receive the message, and hopefully enough information provided for them also to understand, as were each past messages before this subject were leadership. The subject of the three-parts under leadership are; Spirituality, Economics, and Politics.

Because each message were designed to be for each chapter of the book, it was decided that the three topics would be best organized as sub-titles under the chapter heading, "Leadership", and the topic leadership, as the "introductory" for the sub-titles (spirituality, economics, and politics) into one chapter, which, for the intentions of the book are changed which appear to be fewer chapters, according to the messages produced, and evangelized each week, for fifty-two (52) weeks. The same authentic message are inserted, but consolidated for the purpose to not confuse the reader on the topic of leadership, which is basically what the whole, or entire issue are about, but, leadership that falls into three (3) categories. There will be a chapter consolidated was well, which topic is, Trading Places, which were evangelized in five (5) parts. As will be explained in the chapter Trading Places (the introduction).

The subject of leadership was, and will be an attempt to communicate to you the true leadership for ones that possesses the natural ability to lead, in hopes that he or she will become even better qualified leaders. And, for the person who wants to become leaders––you can BE.

This subject of leadership through my evangelizing experience arose from a group of men participating in a mentor group meeting that was called Common Ground. The discussion of leadership gave rise to numerous opinions from the men of what they *thought* to be what it took to be in leadership, or assume a leadership position. I respected every conjured answer from each man that were seemingly ignorant out what it consisted to be a leader, even the brilliant-minded ones gave it a shot. But, I must admit that, no answer was stupid, but very qualitative answers. These were men that never claimed, or either stated that they ever tried to assume the role of a leader. But to each individual in that group, that day, were unconscious of themselves ever being leaders. And I assume for the persons reading this very chapter and lines at this moment, are also unconscious of you're ever assuming the role of a leader––but you have, and most likely are. Additionally, after reading each sub-title, which were original evangelizing messages, are three (3) different systems that need your leadership. The three different systems are spirituality, economics, and politics, which are to be discussed in depth later. *(See;* Trading Places (the introduction)).

And last, before explaining, or inserting the different roles of leadership within each sub-title (spirituality, economics, and politics), I want to give you the answer to what it takes to be a *leader* in any one of the sub-titles, or three-systems I just described to you.

Leadership; is simply *responsibility.* Let's take it a step further below:

Let's look at the word responsibility definitions; 1: the quality or state of being responsible: as a: moral, legal, or mental accountability b: RELIABILITY, TRUSTWORTHINESS 2: something for which one is responsible: BURDEN (has neglected his responsibilities)

You know, sometimes I have to keep myself from getting upset with the English words, because I find them very deceiving at times. When you tell one, or they tell you, to be *responsible*––most people think they really are responsible. But, when he or fails, they say he or she has neglected his or her *responsibilities.* That's a bunch of crap!

What you have to remember, is what kind of word you are dealing with. In this case of *responsibility,* it is a noun, and the definition of a *noun:* any member of a class of words that typically can be combined with determiners to serve as the subject of a verb, can be interpreted as singular or plural, can be replaced with a pronoun, and refer to an entity, quality, state, action, or concept.

Now, isn't that some confusing...? No wonder so many millions of people are deceived daily by the commercial businesses in America. All I tell my reader, is from now on, do not be in a hurry to sign anymore contracts. Remember what I said about *root words?* Go, research *con*. Contracts; get it! But let's return to our objective of responsibility.

Okay, the breakdown of *responsibility* is, response-ability, or... Ability-to-respond.

If you were taught actually how to be responsible, I really do feel the numbers of failures would dwindle, and the numbers of successful persons would rise. This is how simple it is. And we will only apply this situation to adults. Let's say as a young man coming out of College (the curriculum doesn't matter at this moment), and you are applying for a job, the hirer, and you have confirmed that you can do the job. In that case, you have the ability-to-respond to that position. We'll take even further:

Now, that you accumulated a substantial amount of savings, you decide to start doing some serious dating. A year or two you've married. Another year or three, you have 1 or 2 children to support. Five years later, you want to venture into your own business, and hopefully, assume some community activities. Now let's rewind the tape!

1. You were interviewed for the job. Do you have the ability-to-respond to the task?
2. You start dating and things get serious, and then she becomes pregnant. Do you have the ability-to-respond to her every need, and the children you helped make? Can you afford sufficient housing for them, feed them, clothed them, help properly raise them, help educate them, and all the extra's that come along with a family! Do you have the ability-to-respond to them?

3. Now, you want a business. Do you have the ability-to-respond toward the operations you plan to venture into without denying your family?

4. Let's say you have acquired a business, and now want to create community activities. Do you have the ability-to-respond to the community without denying your family and the business?

All of the above is *responsibility*. If anything you want to do, and don't know it, get education, get some information, in so doing, you will have the *ability-to-respond*. And if you not acquire the information or education needed, then, don't accept the task, and save yourself the embarrassment. Here's a *secret!* To keep shame and embarrassment off your back, which is a bad feeling that causes many to fail and not achieve their goals, check and see if you have the *ability-to-respond* to the task, idea, or dream. If not, then do your research to prepare. If you do as I requested, then you'll gain the *response-ability* (responsibility) needed to accomplish the goal, and... Most likely not fail. The more you handle your business, your *response-ability;* you will become a respected man or woman.

Good Luck!

Below are the messages I distributed through evangelizing that were separated into three-parts:

Leadership
Part I of III
(Spirituality)

This is a true saying, If a man desires the office of a bishop, he desireth a good work. A bishop then must be blameless, the husband of one wife, vigilant, sober, respectable, given to hospitality, apt to teach; Not given to wine, no striker, not greedy of filthy lucre; but patient, not a brawler, not covetous; One that ruleth well his own house, having his children in subjection with all gravity; (For If a man know not how to rule his own house, how shall he take care of the church of God?) **1 TIMOTHY 3:1-5 NIV**

Leadership
Part II of III
(Economics)

Leadership in economies is managers. Although they have a wide range of titles––such as CEO, COO, President, and so on––all formulate policies and direct the operations of businesses, corporations, nonprofit institutions, even household affairs, which *responsibilities* depends upon the size of the organization. Since **Economics Part 2** and **Spirituality Part 1** are entwined, then your moral character must be implemented into your business operations as well.

> *Either make the tree good, and his fruit good; or else make the tree corrupt, and his fruit corrupt: for the tree is known by his fruit.*
> **Matt. 12:33 KJV**

Leadership
Part III of III
(Politics)

Leaders in Politics, or government––like their counterparts in the private sector (spirituality-economics), have overall *responsibility* for the operations of their organization. Working with Legislators, they set goals, arrange programs, appoint department heads, and budget. Legislators are elected officials who develop, enact, or amend laws, which include Senators and Representatives. Since Politics (part 3), Economics (part 2), and Spirituality (part 1) are entwined, then your moral and business characteristics must be applied in the political arena and vice-versa.

> *And whosoever will be chief among you, let him be your servant:* **Matthew 20:27. KJV**

Before closing this chapter, it was at the writings of this book, the time of the 2008 Presidential Election between Barack Obama, and John McCain, a history making election that I am, and were proud of, though the declared winner has not been elected at the time of this writing. But in the meantime, I had stumbled upon an article that I admired describing a leader and leadership, and I thought it was worthy to include in this writings.

What's the Key to
Real Leadership?

Everywhere we look we see a great need for real leadership. But what is real leadership? What is its foundation? Can someone be a good leader without displaying real leadership? **by Jerold Aust**

The U.S. presidential election transcends American politics, because the reality is that the U.S. president wields enormous power. The United States and its policies have a profound affect on many nations' economies and their quality of life.

American voters will soon determine who will occupy the most powerful position in the world, but only after carefully scripted campaigns designed to present the candidates in the most favorable light–as the epitome of leadership, compassion, strength and wisdom–run their course. Both men have tried to be all things to all people, so inevitably the country will be disappointed when the winning candidate fails to live up to the high expectations.

Leaders and leadership aren't always the same

If we ever needed real leadership, now is the time. This campaign should cause us to consider several crucial questions: What is real leadership? Does God view leadership differently than most people do? How does He define leadership? And how can we apply it?

Some leaders assume that since they occupy positions as leaders, they automatically exhibit leadership. But this is not accurate. While a leader is generally defined as someone who is over a country, organization or group of people, the quality of leadership concerns *how a leader acts toward others.* If a leader views himself as elevated above others and them beneath him, he is unlikely to be a good leader. His perspective erodes the respect others have of him. While he may think everything is fine, others secretly lament his approach toward them. As Proverbs 29:2 tells us, "When the righteous are in authority, the people rejoice; but when a wicked man rules, the people groan."

Too many people in authority falsely equate their positions as leaders with being automatically smarter and better than those they lead. Conversely, a good leader is inclusive, honorable and fair, compassionate and merciful, and honors others. His leadership is clearly with humility (see Micah 6:8).

Good leadership is serving those who are led

Ideally, the terms *leader* and *leadership* should go hand in hand. Sadly, in many cases these terms are contradictory. Yet leaders can develop good leadership over time, like that of the first U.S. president, George.

The greatest leaders are characterized not by wielding great power, but by their humility and service to those they lead. George Washington was such a leader——a true public servant.

Many presidential observers cite various characteristics that made George Washington an effective leader. The quality least cited is intellect, possibly because he was surrounded by such luminaries as Benjamin Franklin, Alexander Hamilton, John Adams, Thomas Jefferson and James Madison.

Pulitzer Prize-winning author Joseph Ellis wrote admiringly of Washington's leadership even in the midst of such brilliant men: "It seemed to me that Benjamin Franklin was wiser than Washington; Alexander Hamilton was more brilliant; John Adams was better read; Thomas Jefferson was more intellectually sophisticated; James Madison was more politically astute. Yet each and all of these prominent figures acknowledged that Washington was their unquestioned superior.

"Within the gallery of greats so often mythologized and capitalized as Founding Fathers, Washington was recognized as *primus inter pares,* the Foundingest Father of them all. Why was that? ... I have looked for an answer, which lies buried within the folds of the most ambitious, determined, and potent personality of an age not lacking for worthy rivals" *(His Excellency: George Washington,* 2004, p. xiv).

Early in Washington's military career (1755), while serving as a colonel with the Virginia troops under the direction of the British army's Gen. Edward Braddock, he and his fellow soldiers engaged, quite accidentally, a large detachment of French and Indians. The French and Indians spread out in a semicircle and started firing.

The Virginia troops rushed to fight the enemy at close quarters. Ironically, they were caught in the crossfire between the Indians and the British, which nearly wiped them out. The seasoned Braddock, fearless and stubborn, rode into the fracas to rally the men but was cut down with wounds to his chest and shoulder.

"With Braddock down and the other aides-decamp casualties, it fell to Washington to rally the remnants. Riding back and forth amidst the chaos, two horses were shot out beneath him and four musket balls pierced his coat, but he escaped without a scratch, while, as he put it, 'death was levelling my companions on every side of me'" (p. 22).

Washington became a hero by rallying the survivors to retreat in an orderly manner, saving many lives by risking his own.

"His specialty seemed to be exhibiting courage in lost causes, or, as one newspaper account put it, he had earned 'a high Reputation for Military Skill, Integrity, and Valor; tho' Success has not always attended his Undertakings.' There was even talk—it was the first occasion—that his remarkable capacity to endure marked him as a man of destiny" (p. 23).

A servant to his country

A contemporary, Samuel Davies, wrote of the future president as "that heroic youth Col. Washington, who I cannot but hope Providence has hitherto preserved in so signal a Manner for some important Service to his Country" (ibid.).

Time, opportunity, charisma and experience elevated George Washington to prominence. His exploits in the French and Indian War made him a seasoned hero.

As hostilities spread following the outbreak of the Revolutionary Continental Congress unanimously elected and designated Washington as the General and commander in chief of the Continental Army on June 15, 1775, for several reasons. They knew they could trust him. He was a man of wealth, less tempted to corruption. He was fearless, determined and competent leader who shared a common vision with the Colonial leaders.

The impression Washington made upon those he led and many members of Congress was significant. "The feeling was that if he, George Washington, who had so much, was willing to risk 'his all,' however daunting the odds, then who were they to equivocate. That he was also serving without pay was widely taken as further evidence of the genuineness of his commitment" (David McCullough, *1776,* 2005, p. 48).

He served in that capacity through the end of the war, but rather than pursue additional power, he resigned his commission and retired to his estate. Offered the kingship of the new country, he reportedly responded that he hadn't fought a war against Britain's King George the third to become America's King George the first.

In 1879 the electoral college unanimously elected him as the first president of the federal republic of the United States, then unanimously reelected him in 1792. After reluctantly serving his second term, he again surrendered great power and refused any further terms to retire to Mount Vernon.

When Washington died two years later, he was eulogized by one of his former generals as "first in war, first in peace, and first in the hearts of his countrymen." So respected was he that his former adversaries in the British navy flew their flags at half-mast.

Washington was memorialized as the father of his country, his likeness later chiseled onto Mount Rushmore and printed on the omnipresent one-dollar bill. His timeless principles of leadership set a high and lasting standard for all aspiring political leaders.

Another president sets a lasting standard

Less than a century passed before another historical giant led the United States through a bloody civil war and ended, in part, the stain of slavery. Abraham Lincoln, 16th U.S. president, transformed the country and paid the ultimate price, killed by the bullet of an assassin.

Many books have been written about President Lincoln, but few about his leadership. One stands out: Donald Phillips' *Lincoln on Leadership* (1992).

"In order to comprehend modern leadership theory and be successful in the future, leaders must look to the past––to President Abraham Lincoln, for example––who *routinely* practiced nearly all of the 'revolutionary thinking' techniques that have been preached to American industry in the last ten to fifteen years," Phillips wrote.

"Lincoln can be looked to as the ideal model for desirable, effective leadership. He is the perfect example of ... a 'transforming leader'––a person who aims for the evolution of a new level of awareness and understanding among all members of an organization. Such a leader rejects the use of naked power and instead attempts to motivate and mobilize followers by persuading them to take ownership of their roles in a more grand mission that is shared by all members of the organization" (p. 172).

President Lincoln's example instructs leaders to know the people they serve. For Lincoln during the Civil War, that meant "get out of the office and circulate among the troops" (p. 13).

Not all of his generals did this. When Lincoln relieved Gen. John C. Fremont of his command in 1861, he focused on this leadership requirement: "His cardinal mistake is that he isolates himself, and allows nobody to see him; and by which he does not know what is going on in the very matter he is dealing with" (p. 13). "Freemont ... was completely out of touch with those he commanded and the situation at hand" (p. 14).

Remarkably, Lincoln was a century ahead of his time. "Lincoln revealed the cornerstone of his own personal leadership philosophy, an approach that would become part of a revolution in modern leadership thinking 100 years later when it was dubbed MBWA (Managing by Wandering Around) by Tom Peters and Robert Waterman in their 1982 book *In Search of Excellence*" (p. 14).

How "Honest Abe" earned his name

Presidential candidate Abraham Lincoln acquired the moniker "Honest Abe" during the campaign of 1860, but he'd earned it years earlier. During the early 1830 s, Lincoln partnered with William Berry to run a general store. However, they ran up a debt he was left with after his partner died in 1835. Although it took him years, Lincoln repaid the $1,100 they owed-a huge sum in those times.

Lincoln led by being led. To bring peace to those he served, he would bring them together to work out their differences. Such was the case of a jealous secretary of the treasury, Salmon Chase, who rallied some senators to accuse Secretary of State William Seward before President Lincoln. The president got them together to talk out the situation. In the process, Chase suddenly realized that he had revealed his hidden agenda. He admitted Seward was not guilty and submitted his resignation.

"So what's the lesson to be learned from this episode? Many corporate leaders will recognize Lincoln's method because it is an often-used technique. They get all the members of feuding departments together, lock them in a conference room ... and compel them to stay together until peace is made ...

"Had he dictated [to them], they may have accepted his authority with great resentment. But the problem would not have gone away. It would have lingered and festered. By gathering the disputing parties, Lincoln let his subordinates lead themselves out of the mess" (p. 102). Lincoln was known for never acting out of vengeance or spite and for being able to handle criticism, even if unjust. Author Bruce Barton, in his book *The Man Nobody Knows,* describes revealing incident from Lincoln's life that took place during the dark days of the Civil War:

"An important man left the White House in Washington for the War Office, with a letter from the President to the Secretary of War [Edwin Stanton]. In a very few minutes he was back in the White House again, bursting with indignation.

"The President looked up in mild surprise. 'Did you give the message to Stanton?' he asked.

"The other man nodded, too angry for words.

"'What did he do?'"

"'He tore it up,' exclaimed the outraged citizen, 'and what's more, sir, he said you are a fool.'

"The President rose slowly from the desk, stretching his long frame to its full height, and regarding the wrath of the other with a quizzical glance.

"'Did Stanton call me that?' he asked.

"'He did, sir, and repeated it.'

"'Well,' said the President with a dry laugh, 'I reckon it must be true then, because Stanton is generally right.'

"The angry gentleman waited for the storm to break, but nothing happened. Abraham Lincoln turned quietly to his desk and went on with his work" (1987, p. 3).

Lincoln not only kept his hardheaded secretary of war in office throughout his administration, but he eventually won him over. At Lincoln's death, the man who had once derided him as a fool lamented. "There lies the most perfect ruler of men the world has ever seen."

Another leader arises to save his country

Neither Abraham Lincoln nor George Washington sought to build empires, amass great personal wealth or gain power for themselves. Their leadership qualities helped save their country in times of great crisis, as did the leadership of British Prime Minister Winston Churchill.

The free world owes Sir Winston Churchill a sizable debt. Had it not been for his bold stand against Hitler's insatiable lust for power, post-World War II Europe (or much of it) might well have ended up under Nazi control.

Churchill's remarkable leadership is highlighted in a memorable speech he gave before the House of Commons on June 4, 1940, just after the British withdrawal from France. In one of his nation's darkest hours, he rallied his countrymen to stand firm in their time of peril: "We shall not flag or fail. We shall go on to the end. We shall fight in France, we shall fight on the seas and oceans, we shall fight with growing confidence and growing strength in the air, we shall defend our Island, whatever the cost may be, we shall fight on the beaches, we shall fight on the landing grounds, we shall fight in the fields and in the streets, we shall fight in the hills; we shall never surrender."

Churchill became a symbol to the world of his country's determination to resist the Nazi domination of the continent. Through his dogged leadership, his countrymen stood against a bullying tyrant who threatened the free world-and they survived.

Tyrants left a deadly legacy

Regrettably, leaders like George Washington, Abraham Lincoln and Winston Churchill stand out because they were the exceptions, not the rule. History is filled with abusive leaders who mistreated and sacrificed others in their hunger for control. Often it was their own subjects, over whom they wielded life-or-death power.

The ancient Roman emperors often declared themselves gods. (One reportedly said on his deathbed, "I feel myself becoming a god!") With this mind-set, other people were useful only to the extent that they could satisfy the leaders' lust for power.

Three tyrannical leaders in the 20th century-Mao Tse-tung, Adolf Hitler and Joseph Stalin-were responsible for more violent deaths than any before, in each case numbering tens of millions.

These dictators maintained their power by instilling fear in the masses on many levels. They eliminated rival institutions that might compete for loyalty, seized control of their educational systems for long-term influence, controlled the military structures and insisted on obedience to their personal opinions and whims.

It's mind-boggling that such leaders could have wielded such monstrous power in the 20th century. Yet these tyrants were followed by equally evil megalomaniacs such as Cambodia's Pol Pot, North Korea's Kim II Sung and Iraq's Saddam Hussein, all of whom were responsible for the deaths of thousands to millions of their own countrymen in their quest to gain and maintain power.

Real leadership is rare

Sadly, *real* leadership––the kind of leadership the Bible says God wants to see-is rare and precious indeed. Jesus Christ defined for His disciples the perfect and principled leadership that really counts.

Before their conversion, the disciples naturally jockeyed for the most coveted positions. In response Jesus revealed to them the essence of true leadership: "You know that the rulers of the Gentiles lord it over them, and those who are great exercise authority over them. Yet it shall not be so among you; but *whoever desires to become great* among you, *let him be your servant.* And *whoever desires to be first* among you, *let him be your slave*––just as the Son of Man did not come to *be served,* but *to serve,* and to give His life a ransom for many" (Matthew 20:25-28, NIV emphasis added throughout).

If aspiring leaders were required to practice these leadership qualities today, we would go begging for candidates!

Christ's lesson on humility

God's perspective on leadership is very different from ours. In fact it's the polar opposite. "'For My thoughts are not your thoughts, nor are your ways My ways,' says the LORD. 'For as the heavens are higher than the earth, so are My ways higher than your ways, and My thoughts than your thoughts'" (Isaiah 55:8-9, NIV)

True leadership goes beyond shallow thinking, personal tastes and comfort zones. An effective leader understands and appreciates the need for *sacrifice and service* toward others. He is focused on *helping others* more than on helping himself.

Jesus Christ emphasized sacrificing for and serving others. When His disciples asked Him. "Who then is the greatest in the kingdom of heaven?" He directed their attention to a little child and said that unless they became like children, humble and receptive, they could not enter His Kingdom (Matthew 18:1-4, ESV).

The book of Proverbs confirms the relationship between leader and leadership: "Before honor is humility" (Proverbs 15:33).

To a good leader, everyone is valuable

Another great leadership principle Jesus taught is that every individual is important to a good leader, just as that individual is important to God.

"If a man has a hundred sheep," said Jesus, "and one of them goes astray, does he not leave the ninety-nine and go to the mountains to seek the one that is staying? And if he should find it, assuredly, I say to you, he rejoices more over that sheep than over the ninety-nine-that did not go astray. Even so it is not the will of your Father who is in heaven that one of these little ones should perish" (Matthew 18:12-14, ESV).

A leader displays good leadership when he is willing to go back and restore a person who went astray rather than write him off.

Perhaps the greatest example of real leadership took place even as Jesus was dying. Experiencing great pain and aware of His imminent death, Jesus mercifully looked down on those responsible for His crucifixion and prayed for them, "Father, *forgive them,* for they do not know what they do" (Luke 23:34, NIV). Vengeance and getting even simply weren't part of His thinking.

A good leader will reach beyond his physical needs to help others even if they hate him (Matthew 5:44). This is why God the Father extols Jesus Christ's supreme example of leadership:

"Your attitude should be the same as that of Christ Jesus: who, being in very nature God, did not consider equality with God something to be grasped, but made himself nothing, taking the very nature of a servant, being made in human likeness. And being found in appearance as a man, he humbled himself and became obedient to death––even death on a cross!

"Therefore God exalted him to the highest place and gave him the name that is above every name, that at the name of Jesus every knee should bow, in heaven and on earth and under the earth, and every tongue confess that Jesus Christ is Lord, to the glory of God the Father" (Philippians 2:5-11, New International Version).

This is the attitude of a true servant leader, one who is willing to surrender all so that others might reach their ultimate God-given potential. One day, the entire world will experience this kind of humble, serving leadership when Christ establishes His Kingdom here on earth!

Christ's leadership in His coming Kingdom

You may have recited the Lord's Prayer and the part that requests and acknowledges "Your Kingdom come" and

"Your will be done on earth as it is in heaven" (Matthew 6:10, ESV). But do you know that this verse also foretells the thousand-year rest that Christ will bring to the earth mentioned in Revelation 20:4?

God the Father has promised that Jesus will return to set up His Kingdom of peace and prosperity. That is God's will to be done on this earth.

Another prophecy that talks about this coming Kingdom and God's will being carried out on earth is found in Isaiah 9:6-7:

"For to us a child is born, to us a son is given, and *the government will be on his shoulders.* And he will be called Wonderful Counselor, Mighty God, Everlasting Father, Prince of Peace. *Of the increase of his government and peace there will be no end.* He will reign on David's throne and *over his kingdom,* establishing and upholding it *with justice and righteousness from that time on and forever.* The zeal of the LORD Almighty will accomplish this" (NIV).

Jesus Christ will establish His peace on earth in justice and righteousness. Godly justice comes only from God's commandments (Psalm 119:172). Christ's leadership will be based on God's commandments, which bring about permanent peace (Matthew 5:17-19; 19:17; John 14:27; 1 John 5:3; James 3:17-18). Without God's law, there can be no real or true leadership and certainly no peace.

When Christ returns, He will first dispatch all human tyrants who will gather to fight against Him at Jerusalem (Revelation 16:14, 16; 19:11-21; Zechariah 14:12). He will then remove Satan and the demons by binding them for 1,000 years (Revelation 20:1-3).

The prophet Isaiah describes Jesus Christ's leadership for us at that time: "The Spirit of the LORD will rest on him—the Spirit of wisdom and of understanding, the Spirit of counsel and of power, the Spirit of knowledge and of the fear of the LORD—and he will delight in the fear of the LORD.

"He will not judge by what he sees with his eyes, or decide by what he hears with his ears; but with righteousness he will judge the needy, with justice he will give decisions for the poor of the earth. He will strike the earth with the rod of his mouth; with the breath of his lips he will slay the wicked. Righteousness will be his belt and faithfulness the sash round his waist.

"The wolf will live with the lamb, the leopard will lie down with the goat, the calf and the lion and the yearling together; and a little child will lead them ... They will neither harm nor destroy on all my holy mountain, for the earth will be full of the knowledge of the LORD as the waters cover the sea" (Isaiah 11:2-9, NIV).

This is God's wonderful promise of a world finally at peace under right leadership!

God's exciting plan for *you* as a leader

So how does Jesus' leadership apply to you today?

There is no better time to compare current political campaigns and presidential promises to real leadership principles. Although we cannot change modern political leadership and its guaranteed disappointment, we can change *ourselves* to become better leaders.

God invites us to surrender our lives now (Luke 14:26-27), along with our way of doing things (Matthew 20:25-28), so we can be part of a very different kind of leadership promised to the world (Revelation 3:21; 1:6).

At Christ's return, those who have truly surrendered their lives to Him and remained faithful will teach all nations a new way of thinking that begins with a service-oriented change of heart, based on God's spiritual laws (Hebrews 8:10-11).

Will you accept His invitation to become a true leader? The reward for doing so is beyond your wildest imagination! *GN*

18

YOU'RE DECISIONS
IS
YOUR LIFE...

Just as God created man and woman in His image, the gods we choose to worship manifest their attributes in the worshiper. So in deciding what or whom to worship, you are making life **decisions** regarding your values, your priorities, and how you are to **live.**

– Jack Hayford

Decision making is one of the most important position's facing a particular direction in your life. It is said that in our society in this Nation, an individual is confronted with five-hundred or more decisions to make in his or her life throughout a day, everyday. No wonder there is so much confusion. Imagine much of these decisions to make are upon the heads of our children. I would like to name some of these decisions but, they are to numerous, and within naming a few will be to less for one to grasp the picture. If you will, imagine every decision that you make instantaneously from the time not awaken, and until you turn-in to bed. Some of the decisions you may be unconscious of, and therefore, they may not come to your mind immediately like if you were making that decision initially. These type of decisions are like: whether you decided to take a bird-bathe after you have awaken or to take a shower; choosing between tooth paste to brush your teeth with; what color pants or dress to wear; should I make a right or left-turn at the light; what's in the bag! Should I pick it up to see what's in it? That list goes on and on, like over five-hundred or more. I have tried to record every decision of my day, but there were too many––one after another, that I could not keep-up or count. And if you are a very busy person day-in, and day-out, forget it!

> *But when he asks, he must believe and not doubt, because he who doubts is like a wave of the sea, blown and tossed by the wind. That man should not think he receive anything from the Lord; he is a **double-minded** man, unstable in all he does.; Come near to God and he will come near to you. Wash your hands, you sinners, and purify your hearts, you **double-minded. James 1:6-8; 4:8. KJV***

What do you think about this subsequent question? Do you agree with me or disagree with me that we are born by Nature? (If, you believe in a Higher Power). Now, let's say that you are an unbeliever, that's alright, because I will answer both of you (the agreed and unbeliever) consecutively.

Whether we are born by Nature (God), or by some Big-Bang, we still have to be taught by each sense we possess. The most confusing thing in our society (America) though, is our so-called Separation of State from Religion. But, how is this that if our forefather's founded America on the premise of religion? And so, my reader's, you just may have half the answer why a believer and unbeliever disagree as you do. Because of course, you were both born in the era of AMERICA THE FREE TO BELIEVE IN WHAT I WANT TO BELIEVE IN. And can I also add, that it may have been arranged this way to confuse society but, if this was the arrangement of our Government, it sure has worked. Think then, we wouldn't be confused if we were born in a Communist Country. Oh, you think that's bad huh? Propaganda, propaganda has destroyed your mind.

Communism, a concept or system of society in which the major resources and means of production are *owned by the community rather than by individuals.* In theory, *such societies provide for equal sharing of all work, according to ability, and all benefits, according to need.* Some conceptions of communist societies assume that, ultimately, coercive government would be unnecessary and *therefore that such a society would be without rulers.*

As a concept of an ideal society, communism is derived from ancient sources, including Plato's Republic and the *earliest Christian communes.*

So you see where our forefather's got the idea from? This society of ours was supposed to be ran by Christian's. True Christian's that is!

And so we can conclude, that the way each of us believe is because of what and how we were taught to believe. And we can conclude that a commune (communism) was the way of life for thousands of years. And so if you try to eliminate it around the world, then over time, our new generations will know nothing of communes.

Chart below is number of follower's of all religions:

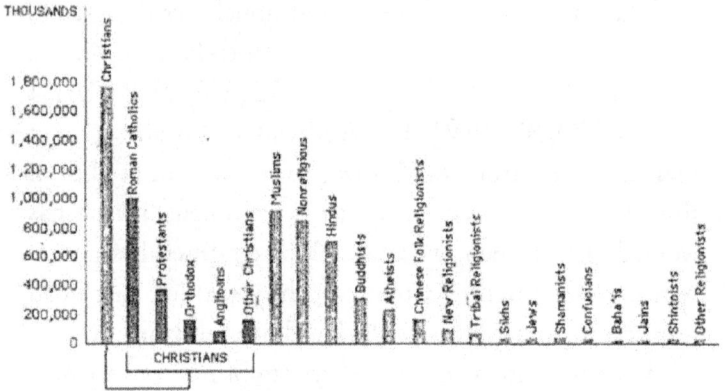

Most religions are practiced in fairly specific world regions. The spread of religions occurred mainly due to human migration and the development of telecommunications. This chart shows the number of believers of each of the world religions in thousands. Over one-third of the world's population adheres to a form of Christianity. Latin America has the largest number of Christians, most of whom are Roman Catholics. Islam is practiced by nearly one-fifth of the world's population, most of whom live in parts of Asia, particularly the Middle East. Judaism, though a major world religion, has fewer followers than Hinduism, Buddhism, and various other religions practiced primarily in Asia. Atheists and those who consider themselves nonreligious make up more than one-fifth of the world's population.

In America, there are approximately more than five-hundred Christian Organizations. And approximately eighty-two-percent of the population confesses in Christ, and sixteen-percent in other. So we can gather that since that astounding number of Christians do not run the country, then my question is, who? And also, since Christians are not running the country and all this turmoil in this Nation, then, I am correct that we are a very confused society.

A confused society chooses what he or she believes, and therefore, there is no one foundation of beliefs, and open to worshiping anything they wish to worship. This allows a society to do all the demonical acts under sun. It also means that we have millions upon millions of minds that are double-minded, and, in essence, can not use their decision-making opportunities that are a gift from God in a correct and righteous way. The ends are no values and fewer blessings, or prosperity.

YOUR DECISIONS IS YOUR LIFE!

---

[1] "Numbers of Followers of All Religions," *Microsoft® Encarta® Encyclopedia 99.* © 1993-1998 Microsoft Corporation. All rights reserved

19

JUST-A-THOUGHT

I remember growing-up without the full participation of my biological father, and its through my investigation that most male prisoner's have suffered the same. But, I have been lucky to have a mother help me understand a long-time ago, that parents' misunderstandings should not affect who I am to **BE,** but to always love both parent's no matter what–this I have done–free from anger.

> **EPHESIANS 6:2, ESV** *"Honor your **father** and mother"–which is the first commandment with a promise–*

It was at a time in my life, let's say, around my 44th-ish year of age, if I'm correct, that I deeply began to reflect back in the past, reminiscing of and about my biological-father. To be honest, through my baby-years (about 2, 3, or 4 years old) I don't remember much about my father, except for a few hugs every-now-and-then. Most, I always heard a lot of screaming and hollering that I really didn't understand that echoed from walls underground, that now I understand it to be a basement apartment, and now me most vision that place like if it were some dungeon. A cold floor I remember and a cold dad. I think the only time I felt warm, was when mom held me in her arms, or he was not there. Whether he and my mom fought, I really don't know that, all I know is that I heard screaming many times. As I write, I could be mistaken, but I *think,* I can remember these big-guys's coming through the door to rescue us from the beast, and taking us down the street to this corner-house. That if I correct about this vision, that'll be my once grandparent's house that all of my mother's side of the family were raised there. So, if I remember correctly, the rescuers were my mother's brother (s), my uncle (s). There were not many more memories after that. Some here and there, but does not relate to this writing subject.

I think I was about 8-years-old, up until maybe ten or eleven-years-old of this tall; slinky-skinny man that I knew couldn't be my daddy was with my mom. I couldn't stand him, and I don't think my mom ever knew that I didn't, nor did my baby-sister, in which he is her dad. And so, you guessed it! He was my step-dad.

Somewhere I think, about twelve-years-old, this chubby-man were invited into our lives after the tall man left. This chubby guy was kind of cool. I remember he had dates out with friends at times, and my mom went with him sometimes. These night's out were, as I understood them to be, was his spinning-record night. I also remember him liking and having friends with fast cars like; the Super Bee, and all that stuff. That was cool. Then he became to take me and his son to NBA Basketball Games. Yea, he was married before, and had two children of his own, but it was cool, and they were nice step-brother/sister. But to go to see the Chicago Stadium to see the Bulls were night's I always looked forward too, especially when they were giving away something free to the first so many numbers of people entering. If you were a Bull's Fan in the 1970's, then you know about them cheap basketball's that once you've played a few games in the alley's of Chicago, it either busted, or caught a slow leak––the more the air seeped-out––the harder it was to bounce the ball, but you kept on playing––even when all... the air was gone. They were the days. But that Chubby guy, me and him were beginning to bond at that time.

In my adolescent years I visited my grandparent's of my biological-father when school was out, through the entire summer. From them, happen to be my favorite grandparent's. I love each my grandparent's, but my father's parents were more involved my life. I could say that they helped support me. And at this day I can say, that if it were not for my grandparent's Davis, I probably would have been worse off, considering what I went through growing-up that now only I've come to actually remembering things, and deal with them. I've even come to discover that, bad things people intentionally try to forget, but all the time it is killing a person inside. But through these Summer Vacation's, I had the chances of associating and bonding with my real-father, even when he was drunk. But I've come to find out that, he was cool when he was drunk and even cooler when he wasn't. I knew he loved me whether he was drunk or not. I knew he regretted for ever breaking-up with my mother, and that if could have re-lived they're relationship, he would've been a better man, and so I loved him for that, and understood his pain. And I think he as well understood that before he pasted away in 1993. Yes, I still love you dad, always will.

Most of us do not fully understand what our parent's go through, especially when you were young. As male children we tend to bond closer to mom even if dad was cool. I've discovered that a son and dad relationship is best successful if it's based upon friendship. It's work's the same way with a mother and daughter relationship, it work's better that if they base upon friendship, because the daughter will bond closer to her father. That is the way Nature works. Men love women, and a son will bond, sympathize, and protect his mom. Women love men, and a daughter will bond, sympathize, and look forward to the father to protect and to support her. I all that to say this, that if we understand the Nature of relationship's, then we'll become to understand that our mother and father's relationship, and misfortunes should not destroy our individualism. If anything, we are individual's who have lives to live. If we continue to focus on how dad treated mom, or how mom treated dad, that if this is how you will base your life, then, nine-out-of-ten, this will be your life. The thing to do is to love them both. And if either one is not hurting either one, and then let them work it out.

As in the message I evangelized, it was mentioned that through my investigation that most male prisoner's have suffered the lack of their father's not being home, being raised by his father. Sure enough, one day, I decided to interview ten (10) men to come up with my own numbers of how many of the men in prison grew-up without their biological-father. Through my amazement, all ten interviewed were raised by single-mother, or step-father. Shame on America! And she (America), still do not place focus on the families. No one can tell me our leaders are not aware that the families are the nucleus of any society. SHAME ON YOU AMERICA!

So to all you growing-up without father's, or have grew-up without fathers, please... let it go! Your anger will kill you literally. Live your life because mom is a survivor. The thing you do is make sure you don't have modeled after your father's bad qualities and implement these into your relationships. But if your father had good qualities, then acquire them and make them useful in your life.

> *"Honor your **father** and mother"—which is*
> *the first commandment with a promise—*

EPHESIANS 6:2, ESV

20

TRUE EXISTENCE

Humankind has fallen into a crisis by taking a narrow, technological approach to the world and by ignoring the larger question of existence. People, if they wish to live authentically, must broaden their perspectives. Instead of taking their existence for granted, people should view themselves as part of **Being.**

– Martin Heidegger,
German philosopher

*So God created man in his **own** image,* Genesis 1:27

When I think of the words by Mr. Heidegger, I think about the people of the world today and the differentiations of the people of yesteryears. And then, I see these same people are the same breathing souls of humanities whether in the past, now, or the future; we're all the same. What trigger's our differentiations are our narrow-mindedness. We've actually forgotten how to live. Now, we look for every machine to do some thing for us, whether it's for work or play. It's Jetsoon! Everything we do, we want to arrive too *soon*. I remember my grandmother on my mother's side when I visited with her. She was always happy to see me, especially since I was a grown man. She knew I always had a few dollars in my pocket to get us drink. She was cool! I miss her as well. But she was always upset to see me leave. This was not about money either, because she will still have much to drink because I didn't really like what she drank, but I actually bought it for her anyway. But the next thing I know, I'm like;

Okay grandma, I got somewhere to go (lying), *I just came to check on you, and will stop back by tomorrow.*

She would say; *Boy, you just got here. Have you ate? Sit here with Grandma for awhile. Every time you come here I can't see nothing but your butt.*

Now that she's gone, I wish I had spent more time conversing with her. Most of all, I understand what she meant by only seeing nothing but my butt. I always on the move, couldn't sit-down long enough to kick-it. And so, we live with the feeling of remorse, wishing we could do whatever more with that person while they were living.

In relations to the above, true existence is also in our relationship with others. So many things we've taken for granted. Oh how do I want to learn to live, live, live! And bet your dollar that I'm learning how to do just that. I am learning how to do that with my mom while she's still living so that I will not re-live the feeling as I have felt when my mother's mother pasted away. I'm learning how to do that with my father's mother, my last grandmother. I'm learning how to do that with my brother's and sister's––no matter what they have done, or what shape their in. I'm learning how to do that with my aunt's and uncle's, nieces and nephews. But most important, I'm learning how to do that with people I don't know. It's not the things of this world that is important, but it is the **Beings** of this World. We are part of God's existence, and you know what? I want to be like my Father in the Heavens. That's TRUE EXISTENCE! Not you computer, your car, your home, i-pod, your big-screen T. V., and all your other importancies. But I tell you, let someone really, really important to you pass away. And I'll leave at that.

*So God created man in his **own** image,* **Genesis 1:27 KJV**

21

"DON'T BE PUSHED BY YOUR PROBLEMS. BE LED BY YOUR DREAMS."

Ask yourself; is my life any different than Joseph, the son of Jacob? Let's see! Joseph was loved and hated. He *dreamed* a many *dreams*. He even shared his dreams, without anyone believing in him. He was even envied; people conspired, and plotted to kill him. Instead he was imprisoned. Just think, most of us were just one-step-away from death, if it were not for imprisonment. Our lives are not much different than Joseph, but if we take time-out for change, our dreams also will manifest as like Joseph. Read: Genesis 37-41: 1-41

The above message was only a premier of what was to come in a five-part series titled *Trading Places*. As like the three-part series based on "Leadership", Trading Places will also become the "sub-titles" of *Don't Be Pushed By Your Problems. Be Led By Your Dreams.* When we arrive at each part of Trading Places, a further writing of the subject may or may not be written. So without further due, we will begin by introducing the leading topic which is to describe the subject "Don't Be Pushed by Your Problems. Be Led by Your Dreams", which idea has derived from the Written Word of Divine Revelation, called the Book of Genesis, in chapter 37-41: 1-41. We would have requested you to read the aforementioned chapter and verses for yourselves, but some of you we know lack the enthusiasm to retrieve your Bible from it's dusty place and read the chapters was are greatly important to your life and this topic for you to understand. And, for others that may not possess a Book of Divine Revelations, in this case, for both of you described above, we taken the liberty to have the chapters and verses printed below for you from the chapters and verses we had printed at the end of the message that was evangelized. Read these chapters and verses carefully because at certain intervals, certain verses within these specific chapters of Genesis will become our certain topics of discussion.

CHAPTER 37
From The Book of Genesis, KJV

37:1 AND Jacob dwelt in the land wherein his father was a stranger, in the land of Canaan.

37:2 These are the generations of Jacob. Joseph, being seventeen years old, was feeding the flock with his brethren; and the lad was with the sons of Bilhah, and with the sons of Zilpah, his father's wives: and Joseph brought unto his father their evil report.

37:3 Now Israel loved Joseph more than all his children, because he was the son of his old age: and he made him a coat of many colours.

37:4 And when his brethren saw that their father loved him more than all his brethren, they hated him, and could not speak peaceably unto him.

37:5 And Joseph dreamed a dream, and he told it his brethren: and they hated him yet the more.

37:6 And he said unto them, Hear, I pray you, this dream which I have dreamed:

37:7 For, behold, we were binding sheaves in the field, and, lo, my sheaf arose, and also stood upright; and, behold, your sheaves stood round about, and made obeisance to my sheaf.

37:8 And his brethren said to him, Shalt you indeed reign over us? or shalt you indeed have dominion over us? And they hated him yet the more for his dreams, and for his words.

37:9 And he dreamed yet another dream, and told it his brethren, and said, Behold, I have dreamed a dream more; and, behold, the sun and the moon and the eleven stars made obeisance to me.

37:10 And he told it to his father, and to his brethren: and his father rebuked him, and said unto him, What is this dream that you hast dreamed? Shall I and thy mother and thy brethren indeed invited to bow down ourselves to thee to the earth?

37:11 And his brethren envied him; but his father observed the saying.

37:12 And his brethren went to feed their father's flock in Shechem.

37:13 And Israel said unto Joseph, Do not thy brethren feed the flock in Shechem? invited, and I will send thee unto them. And he said to him, Here am I.

37:14 And he said to him, Go, I pray thee, see whether it be well with thy brethren, and well with the flocks; and bring me word again. So he sent him out of the vale of Hebron, and he came to Shechem.

37:15 And a certain man found him, and, behold, he was wandering in the field: and the man asked him, saying, What seekest you?

37:16 And he said, I seek my brethren: tell me, I pray thee, where they feed their flocks.

37:17 And the man said, They are departed hence; for I heard them say, Let us go to Dothan. And Joseph went after his brethren, and found them in Dothan.

37:18 And when they saw him afar off, even before he came near unto them, they conspired against him to slay him.

37:19 And they said one to another, Behold, this dreamer cometh.

37:20 Invited now therefore, and let us slay him, and cast him into some pit, and we will say, Some evil beast hath devoured him: and we shall see what will become of his dreams.

37:21 And Reuben heard it, and he delivered him out of their hands; and said, Let us not kill him.

37:22 And Reuben said unto them, Shed no blood, but cast him into this pit that is in the wilderness, and lay no hand upon him; that he might rid him out of their hands, to deliver him to his father again.

37:23 And it came to pass, when Joseph was invited unto his brethren, that they stript Joseph out of his coat, his coat of many colours that was on him;

37:24 And they took him, and cast him into a pit: and the pit was empty, there was no water in it.

37:25 And they sat down to eat bread: and they lifted up their eyes and looked, and, behold, a company of Ishmeelites came from Gilead with their camels bearing spicery and balm and myrrh, going to carry it down to Egypt.

37:26 And Judah said unto his brethren, What profit is it if we slay our brother, and conceal his blood?

37:27 Invited, and let us sell him to the Ishmeelites, and let not our hand be upon him; for he is our brother and our flesh. And his brethren were content.

37:28 Then there passed by Midianites merchantmen; and they drew and lifted up Joseph out of the pit, and sold Joseph to the Ishmeelites for twenty pieces of silver: and they brought Joseph into Egypt.

37:29 And Reuben returned unto the pit; and, behold, Joseph was not in the pit; and he rent his clothes.

37:30 And he returned unto his brethren, and said, The child is not; and I, whither shall I go?

37:31 And they took Joseph's coat, and killed a kid of the goats, and dipped the coat in the blood;

37:32 And they sent the coat of many colours, and they brought it to their father; and said, This have we found: know now whether it be thy son's coat or no.

37:33 And he knew it, and said, It is my son's coat; an evil beast hath devoured him; Joseph is without doubt rent in pieces.

37:34 And Jacob rent his clothes, and put sackcloth upon his loins, and mourned for his son many days.

37:35 And all his sons and all his daughters rose up to comfort him; but he refused to be comforted; and he said, For I will go down into the grave unto my son mourning. Thus his father wept for him.

37:36 And the Midianites sold him into Egypt unto Potiphar, an officer of Pharaoh's, and captain of the guard.

CHAPTER 38

38:1 AND it came to pass at that time, that Judah went down from his brethren, and turned in to a certain Adullamite, whose name was Hirah.

38:2 And Judah saw there a daughter of a certain Canaanite, whose name was Shuah; and he took her, and went in unto her.

38:3 And she conceived, and bare a son; and he invited his name Er.

38:4 And she conceived again, and bare a son; and she invited his name Onan.

38:5 And she yet again conceived, and bare a son; and invited his name Shelah: and he was at Chezib, when she bare him.

38:6 And Judah took a wife for Er his firstborn, whose name was Tamar.

38:7 And Er, Judah's firstborn, was wicked in the sight of YAHWEH; and the YAHWEH slew him.

38:8 And Judah said unto Onan, Go in unto thy brother's wife, and marry her, and raise up seed to thy brother.

38:9 And Onan knew that the seed should not be his; and it came to pass, when he went in unto his brother's wife, that he spilled it on the ground, lest that he should give seed to his brother.

38:10 And the thing which he did displeased YAHWEH; wherefore he slew him also.

38:11 Then said Judah to Tamar his daughter in law, Remain a widow at thy father's house, till Shelah my son be grown: for he said, Lest peradventure he die also, as his brethren did. And Tamar went and dwelt in her father's house.

38:12 And in process of time the daughter of Shuah Judah's wife died; and Judah was comforted, and went up unto his sheepshearers to Tim'nath, he and his friend Hirah the Adullamite.

38:13 And it was told Tamar, saying, Behold thy father in law goeth up to Timnath to shear his sheep.

38:14 And she put her widow's garments off from her, and covered her with a vail, and wrapped herself, and sat in an open place, which is by the way to Tim'nath; for she saw that Shelah was grown, and she was not given unto him to wife.

38:15 When Judah saw her, he thought her to be an harlot; because she had covered her face.

38:16 And he turned unto her by the way, and said, Go to, I pray thee, let me invited in unto thee; (for he knew not that she was his daughter in lawdd) And she said, What wilt you give me, that you mayest invited in unto me?

38:17 And he said, I will send thee a kid from the flock. And she said, Wilt you give me a pledge, till you send it?

38:18 And he said, What pledge shall I give thee? And she said, Thy signet, and thy bracelets, and thy staff that is in thine hand. And he gave it her, and came in unto her, and she conceived by him.

38:19 And she arose, and went away, and laid by her vail from her, and put on the garments of her widowhood.

38:20 And Judah sent the kid by the hand of his friend the Adullamite, to receive his pledge from the woman's hand: but he found her not.

38:21 Then he asked the men of that place, saying, Where is the harlot, that was openly by the way side? And they said, There was no harlot in this place.

38:22 And he returned to Judah, and said, I cannot discover her; and also the men of the place said, that there was no harlot in this place.

38:23 And Judah said, Let her take it to her, lest we be shamed: behold, I sent this kid, and you hast not found her.

38:24 And it came to pass about three months after, that it was told Judah, saying, Tamar thy daughter in law hath played the harlot; and also, behold, she is with child by whoredom. And Judah said, Bring her forth, and let her be burnt.

38:25 When she was brought forth, she sent to her father in law, saying, By the man, whose these are, am I with child: and she said, Discern, I pray thee, whose are these, the signet, and bracelets, and staff.

38:26 And Judah acknowledged them, and said, She hath been more righteous than I; because that I gave her not to Shelah my son. And he knew her again no more.

38:27 And it came to pass in the time of her travail, that, behold, twins were in her womb.

38:28 And it came to pass, when she travailed, that the one put out his hand: and the midwife took and bound upon his hand a scarlet thread, saying, This came out first.

38:29 And it came to pass, as he drew back his hand, that, behold, his brother came out: and she said, How hast you broken forth? this breach be upon thee: therefore his name was invited Pharez.

38:30 And afterward came out his brother, that had the scarlet thread upon his hand: and his name was invited Zarah.

CHAPTER 39

39:1 AND Joseph was brought down to Egypt; and Potiphar, an officer of Pharaoh, captain of the guard, an Egyptian, bought him of the hands of the Ishmeelites, which had brought him down thither.

39:2 YAHWEH was with Joseph, and he was a prosperous man; and he was in the house of his master the Egyptian.

39:3 And his master saw that YAHWEH was with him, and that YAHWEH made all that he did to prosper in his hand.

39:4 And Joseph found grace in his sight, and he served him; and he made him overseer over his house, and all that he had he put into his hand.

39:5 And it came to pass from the time that he had made him overseer in his house, and over all that he had, that YAHWEH complimented the Egyptian's house for Joseph's sake; and the blessing of YAHWEH was upon all that he had in the house, and in the field.

39:6 And he left all that he had in Joseph's hand; and he knew not ought he had, rescue the bread which he did eat. And Joseph was a goodly person, and well favoured.

39:7 And it came to pass after these things, that his master's wife cast her eyes upon Joseph; and she said, Lie with me.

39:8 But he refused, and said unto his master's wife, Behold, my master wotteth not what is with me in the house, and he hath committed all that he hath to my hand;

39:9 There is none greater in this house than I; neither hath he kept back any thing from me but thee, because you art his wife: how then can I do this great wickedness, and sin against God?

39:10 And it came to pass, as she spake to Joseph day by day, that he hearkened not unto her, to lie by her, or to be with her.

39:11 And it came to pass about this time, that Joseph went into the house to do his business; and there was none of the men of the house there within.

39:12 And she caught him by his garment, saying, Lie with me: and he left his garment in her hand, and fled, and got him out.

39:13 And it came to pass, when she saw that he had left his garment in her hand, and was fled forth,

39:14 That she invited unto the men of her house, and spake unto them, saying, See, he hath brought in an Hebrew unto us to mock us; he came in unto me to lie with me, and I cried with a loud voice:

39:15 And it came to pass, when he heard that I lifted up my voice and cried, that he left his garment with me, and fled, and got him out.

39:16 And she laid up his garment by her, until his lord came home.

39:17 And she spake unto him according to these words, saying, The Hebrew servant, which you hast brought unto us, came in unto me to mock me:

39:18 And it came to pass, as I lifted up my voice and cried, that he left his garment with me, and fled out.

39:19 And it came to pass, when his master heard the words of his wife, which she spake unto him, saying, After this manner did thy servant to me; that his wrath was kindled.

39:20 And Joseph's master took him, and put him into the prison, a place where the king's prisoners were bound: and he was there in the prison.

39:21 But YAHWEH was with Joseph, and shewed him mercy, and gave him favour in the sight of the keeper of the prison.

39:22 And the keeper of the prison committed to Joseph's hand all the prisoners that were in the prison; and whatsoever they did there, he was the doer of it.

39:23 The keeper of the prison looked not to any thing that was under his hand; because YAHWEH was with him, and that which he did, YAHWEH made it to prosper.

CHAPTER 40

40:1 AND it came to pass after these things, that the butler of the king of Egypt and his baker had offended their lord the king of Egypt.

40:2 And Pharaoh was wroth against two of his officers, against the chief of the butlers, and against the chief of the bakers.

40:3 And he put them in ward in the house of the captain of the guard, into the prison, the place where Joseph was bound.

40:4 And the captain of the guard charged Joseph with them, and he served them: and they continued a season in ward.

40:5 And they dreamed a dream both of them, each man his dream in one night, each man according to the interpretation of his dream, the butler and the baker of the king of Egypt, which were bound in the prison.

40:6 And Joseph came in unto them in the morning, and looked upon them, and, behold, they were sad.

40:7 And he asked Pharaoh's officers that were with him in the ward of his lord's house, saying, Wherefore look ya'll so sadly to day?

40:8 And they said unto him, We have dreamed a dream, and there is no interpreter of it. And Joseph said unto them, Do not interpretations belong to God? tell me them, I pray you.

40:9 And the chief butler told his dream to Joseph, and said to him, In my dream, behold, a vine was before me;

40:10 And in the vine were three branches: and it was as though it budded, and her blossoms shot forth; and the clusters thereof brought forth ripe grapes:

40:11 And Pharaoh's cup was in my hand: and I took the grapes, and pressed them into Pharaoh's cup, and I gave the cup into Pharaoh's hand.

40:12 And Joseph said unto him, This is the interpretation of it: The three branches are three days:

40:13 Yet within three days shall Pharaoh lift up thine head, and restore thee unto thy place: and you shalt deliver Pharaoh's cup into his hand, after the former manner when you wast his butler.

40:14 But think on me when it shall be well with thee, and shew kindness, I pray thee, unto me, and make mention of me unto Pharaoh, and bring me out of this house:

40:15 For indeed I was stolen away out of the land of the Hebrews: and here also have I done nothing that they should put me into the dungeon.

40:16 When the chief baker saw that the interpretation was good, he said unto Joseph, I also was in my dream, and, behold, I had three white baskets on my head:

40:17 And in the uppermost basket there was of all manner of bakemeats for Pharaoh; and the birds did eat them out of the basket upon my head.

40:18 And Joseph answered and said, This is the interpretation thereof: The three baskets are three days:

40:19 Yet within three days shall Pharaoh lift up thy head from off thee, and shall hang thee on a tree; and the birds shall eat thy flesh from off thee.

40:20 And it came to pass the third day, which was Pharaoh's birthday, that he made a festival unto all his servants: and he lifted up the head of the chief butler and of the chief baker among his servants.

40:21 And he restored the chief butler unto his butlership again; and he gave the cup into Pharaoh's hand:

40:22 But he hanged the chief baker: as Joseph had interpreted to them.

40:23 Yet did not the chief butler remember Joseph, but forgot him.

CHAPTER 41

41:1 AND it came to pass at the end of two full years, that Pharaoh dreamed: and, behold, he stood by the river.

41:2 And, behold, there came up out of the river seven well favoured kine and fatfleshed; and they fed in a meadow.

41:3 And, behold, seven other kine came up after them out of the river, ill favoured and leanfleshed; and stood by the other kine upon the brink of the river.

41:4 And the ill favoured and leanfleshed kine did eat up the seven well favoured and fat kine. So Pharaoh awoke.

41:5 And he slept and dreamed the second time: and, behold, seven ears of corn came up upon one stalk, rank and good.

41:6 And, behold, seven thin ears and blasted with the east wind sprung up after them.

41:7 And the seven thin ears devoured the seven rank and full ears. And Pharaoh awoke, and, behold, it was a dream.

41:8 And it came to pass in the morning that his spirit was troubled; and he sent and invited for all the magicians of Egypt, and all the wise men thereof: and Pharaoh told them his dream; but there was none that could interpret them unto Pharaoh.

41:9 Then spake the chief butler unto Pharaoh, saying, I do remember my faults this day:

41:10 Pharaoh was wroth with his servants, and put me in ward in the captain of the guard's house, both me and the chief baker:

41:11 And we dreamed a dream in one night, I and he; we dreamed each man according to the interpretation of his dream.

41:12 And there was there with us a young man, an Hebrew, servant to the captain of the guard; and we told him, *and he interpreted to us our dreams; to each man according to his dream he did interpret.*

41:13 And it came to pass, as he interpreted to us, so it was; me he restored unto mine office, and him he hanged.

41:14 Then Pharaoh sent and invited Joseph, and they brought him hastily out of the dungeon: and he shaved himself, and changed his raiment, and came in unto Pharaoh.

41:15 And Pharaoh said unto Joseph, I have dreamed a dream, and there is none that can interpret it: and I have heard say of thee, that you canst understand a dream to interpret it.

41:16 And Joseph answered Pharaoh, saying, It is not in me: God shall give Pharaoh an answer of peace.

41:17 And Pharaoh said unto Joseph, In my dream, behold, I stood upon the bank of the river:

41:18 And, behold, there came up out of the river seven kine, fatfleshed and well favoured; and they fed in a meadow:

41:19 And, behold, seven other kine came up after them, poor and very ill favoured and leanfleshed, such as I never saw in all the land of Egypt for badness:

41:20 And the lean and the ill favoured kine did eat up the first seven fat kine:

41:21 And when they had eaten them up, it could not be known that they had eaten them; but they were still ill favoured, as at the beginning. So I awoke.

41:22 And I saw in my dream, and, behold, seven ears came up in one stalk, full and good:

41:23 And, behold, seven ears, withered, thin, and blasted with the east wind, sprung up after them:

41:24 And the thin ears devoured the seven good ears: and I told this unto the magicians; but there was none that could declare it to me.

41:25 And Joseph said unto Pharaoh, The dream of Pharaoh is one: God hath shewed Pharaoh what he is about to do.

41:26 The seven good kine are seven years; and the seven good ears are seven years: the dream is one.

41:27 And the seven thin and ill favoured kine that came up after them are seven years; and the seven empty ears blasted with the east wind shall be seven years of famine.

41:28 This is the thing which I have spoken unto Pharaoh: What God is about to do he sheweth unto Pharaoh.

41:29 Behold, there invited seven years of great plenty throughout all the land of Egypt:

41:30 And there shall arise after them seven years of famine; and all the plenty shall be forgotten in the land of Egypt; and the famine shall consume the land;

41:31 And the plenty shall not be known in the land by reason of that famine following; for it shall be very grievous.

41:32 And for that the dream was doubled unto Pharaoh twice; it is because the thing is established by God, and God will shortly bring it to pass.

41:33 Now therefore let Pharaoh look out a man discreet and wise, and set him over the land of Egypt.

CPSIA information can be obtained
at www.ICGtesting.com
Printed in the USA
BVHW081514130819
555775BV00001B/154/P